To Dian

God bless you

as you serve

Him.

Rick Jones

Seasons of A Pastor

Richard Jones

authorHOUSE®

AuthorHouse™
1663 Liberty Drive, Suite 200
Bloomington, IN 47403
www.authorhouse.com
Phone: 1-800-839-8640

First published by AuthorHouse   4/28/2009

Printed in the United States of America
Bloomington, Indiana
This book is printed on acid-free paper.

ISBN: 978-1-4389-2912-5 (sc)

Acknowledgements

The journey that led to this book actually began over 25 years ago when I started journaling on a regular basis. I actually began organizing entries for the purpose of this project almost three years ago. Writing began the summer of 2006. I believe it to be no accident that the culmination of the project comes at another pivotal transition in my own life. I have recently stepped down (this month to be exact) from a staff position from the church which I have served for 30 years. I continue to work as an employee of the LaPorte Community School Corporation in LaPorte, Indiana, as well as a private tutor.

I wish to acknowledge some special individuals who have been especially encouraging during the course of bringing this work to completion. Special thanks to Donna Hale (teacher at Lincoln Elementary) for her hours of proofing and counsel regarding my manuscript. Thanks to Marty Briggs (teacher at Crichfield Elementary) and his assistant Jane Hubner for their reading and suggestions. Thanks to my best friend, Greg Weiler for his reading and enthusiasm for the project, and to Darlene Mannix, a published writer who has encouraged me along the way. And thank you, Lynn for the neat wall plaque; it sits right next to my writing computer. Thank you to Mark Bublitz and Rob Lula for your special encouragement gift; it was overwhelming! I am grateful to my pastor, Kevin Galloway for his friendship and prayers; it's cool after 40 plus years to actually have my own pastor. Thanks to my dad, Warren Jones, for his role-modeling of what a father should be. And especially I thank my bride, Helen, of 42 years for the support and positive spirit she has continuously given to me in this writing. I truly believe that this experience has prepared me for the next leg of my personal journal in the years ahead.

Richard Jones

June, 2008

I dedicate this book to my precious family
(To Helen, Dad, Chris & Tim, Becky & Joel, and Jessie,
Grace, Chloe,
Christian, Caryn, & TJ)
And
To my awesome God-children, Heather and Miles

Forward

I first met Rick Jones in the winter of 1992. At the time he was the Senior Pastor of Countryside Christian Church, and I was a young police officer who had been given the assignment of investigating an auto crash involving members of Rick's church family. This crash, which resulted in the death of a church member, occurred in front of the church building right before a worship service. Needless to say, there was much chaos, grief, and pain. I remember watching Rick pray with a family at the hospital while I waited to speak with those involved. I remember watching him care and love his friends. Rick had no clue that I was watching and didn't remember meeting me then. Although I did not know these people, I felt cared for and safe in that moment.

This is what a shepherd does. This is the work of a pastor. Rick is a pastor.

Eleven years later, I met Rick for a second time. This meeting involved Rick interviewing me for the position of Worship Pastor at Countryside, which eventually led to Rick and I working closely together for two years. During this time, Rick and I faced much adversity and trial together. When I was discouraged, Rick encouraged. When I need correcting, Rick corrected. When I needed to be told no, Rick said no. When our family needed reassuring, Rick pointed us to Jesus. When my wife needed a smile, Helen was there to bring joy. Rick was not just my friend and my boss, he was my pastor. I can honestly say, Rick has been the only true pastor in my life and continues to be to this date.

In September of 2006, I had the honor of commissioning Rick in his next season of ministry with children. Praying over Rick and Helen was one of the most humbling things I have ever had the honor of doing in ministry. This occurred on the day that Rick passed the baton of leadership to me and commissioned me to my new season of ministry as Lead Pastor. I will never forget that day. You see, on this day I found Rick kneeling down to console a small child who had fallen down and scraped her knee. I watched Rick love and care for this child. Rick had no clue that I was watching nor that anyone else was around to see. And, once again I found myself feeling cared for and safe in that moment. This is what a shepherd does. This is the work of a pastor. I am proud to say that Rick Jones is my pastor.

What you are about to read are the lessons learned from over 40 years of ministry. The pages are rich with knowledge, wisdom, and grace. I feel lucky to have had some of this wisdom passed on to me as I have worked with Rick. My prayer is that all whose lives have been touch by the Jones' ministry would find a renewed passion for the glory of God and a renewed thankfulness for His servants such as Rick. May God continue to bless Rick in this season of ministry. May God bless you.

Kevin Galloway

September 2008

Introduction

"When I have ceased to break my wings
against the faultiness of things;
And learned that compromises wait
behind each hardly opened gate;
When I can look life in the eyes,
grown calm and very coldly wise;
Life will have given me the truth
and taken in exchange my youth.
(Sara Teasdale)

Proverbs 3 daily reminds me of that truth which I have continued to learn—*Blessed is the man who finds wisdom, the man who gains understanding, for she is more profitable than silver and yields better returns than gold. She is more precious than rubies; nothing you desire can compare with her.* (Vv 13-15)

D. L. Moody used to say, "I have had more trouble with myself than with any other man." A.W. Tozer wrote, "May not the inadequacy of much of our spiritual experience be traced back to our habit of skipping through the corridors of the Kingdom like children through the marketplace, chattering about everything, but pausing to learn the true value of nothing." I think that has been a great fear of mine for years.

I am not a spiritual giant; I find it hard to identify with spiritual giants. I read through the gospels and totally identify with the disciples of Jesus and how unspiritual they were. I love the disciples...they remind me of me. I think the summary of

Jesus' teachings to them (and to us) is "You're going to outlive 'life'...Don't take too good care of yourself...Find the things that count...Stick your neck out...Spill some blood...Spread some love...The sin is not always in breaking the rules; it's in holding back."

And I am not a contemplative. I'm just a man who wants to be serious with God. I've worked hard over the years not to take myself too seriously. Sometimes I've succeeded; sometimes not. I am well aware of the fact that God did quite well before I showed up and He will do quite nicely after I'm gone. But I've still struggled with so much stuff in my ministry. Stuff like, why is it that when the apostle Paul preached there was a revolution? When I preach people rush out for coffee and donuts. Why is it that when Paul proclaimed Jesus, he got thrown in jail, beaten up, whipped and even stoned? When I preach Jesus, people walk up and say, "Good sermon, Rick," and then go to Ryan's all you can eat buffet for dinner.

This book has been developed from my personal journals. I've been journaling for many years; I've lost track of exactly how many. They are notebooks of thoughts, schedules, questions and sometimes garbage (which needs to be dumped somewhere). Sometimes I think that through the years my journals have served as my personal "psychiatrist's couch".

It's interesting how I've mastered the art of hiding my inner self from others around me (sometimes even my wife). I have always kept a lot inside of myself so that no one can discern who I really am. But I need to tell and to share and to unload. I need to bare my soul, but to whom? Of course the religiously correct answer is "the Lord". I have been able to more effectively do that through the tool of my journals. I write in my journal and it never offers comment or suggestion or criticism or judgment. It just stares back and will eat as many words as I feed it. This kind of writing has blessed my life greatly over the years.

"I know not what is happening in my ministry. I know not the future. I only know that in Christ I am at peace." (Personal journal – September 26, 1990)

There has been a lot of discussion on this whole matter of "the call" to ministry. I've had pastors work with me who did not believe in a specific calling. I absolutely reject that thinking. I remember (as if it were yesterday) God calling me to be a pastor the summer of 1961. I was a sophomore in high school. When I think of that evening on the campus of Lincoln Christian College in Lincoln, Illinois, I still get teary-eyed. An invitation was given that evening for any who felt the leading of the Lord to go into the pastoral ministry. I remember the speaker saying, "The preachers are coming! The preachers are coming!" I believe to this day that I actually heard the voice of God saying to me, "GO!" I don't remember walking up to the front; but all of sudden I found myself there, sobbing uncontrollably. That was my "non-calling" to the ministry experience.

In this volume it is my humble desire to analyze 40 plus years in the pastoral ministry from the perspective of God changing me. Deeper than simply "lessons I've learned", I guess I share in light of "things I wish I would have known" – "things I wish I would have had the courage to say or do" – "principles I wish I would have started living sooner." I could have titled this book, *Things I Have Learned Since I Knew Everything.* Each chapter will be a comparison of priorities. These chapters will detail what I struggle to make real in my life today. They will reveal what I wish I would have started living a long time ago. I guess I was like the guy Stephen Brown talks about in his *Key Life* radio broadcasts. I've come to the realization that through much of my ministry I had the words right but I missed the tune. And if you miss the tune you miss the awesomeness of the whole song. I do not wish to skip "through the corridors of the Kingdom like children through the marketplace." I can tell you at the outset that the giant step in my walk of faith is the one I took when I decided that God was no longer a part of my life—HE IS MY LIFE.*!!*

Chapter One – Love over Law

Probably one the greatest principles that I wished I would have started living sooner is this one—LOVE OVER LAW. I still regress; but this truth has literally begun to take over my life.

Did you know that in Indiana, hotel sheets must be exactly 99 inches long and 81 inches wide? Were you aware that if any person has a puppet show, wire dancing or a tumbling act in the state and receives money for it, they will be fined $3 under the Act to Prevent Certain Immoral Practices? Did you know that Indiana's books still proclaim (this was actually passed as a law) that the value of Pi is 3? Also, a man over the age of 18 may be arrested for statutory rape if the passenger in his car is not wearing her socks and shoes, and is under the age of 17. Indiana law also states that it is against the law for a liquor store to sell milk, you can get out of paying for a dependent's medical care by praying for him, and baths may not be taken between the months of October and March. (Dumb.com/ Silly Laws/Indiana) Ridiculous? Surprisingly, they are still on the books. Yet there are equally surprising and equally ridiculous things that people still put up with in the name of holiness and propriety within the church of Jesus Christ. I find it amazing that we as a nation will fight and sacrifice lives so our country and others can be free, but when it comes to living out our Christianity we will give up our freedom without a battle. There are those all around us with the "spiritual" gift of criticism who will attempt to butcher our walk and experience in Christ because of their take on what being a Christian is all about and will devote their considerable abilities and energies

1

to critiquing our walk with the Lord. The apostle Paul tells us over and over again to watch out for them. Watch out for those who will never miss a chance to stir things up and who will readily destroy your joy by sucking you into debate over music and sermons and dress and hair style and whatever. Paul in the opening of Philippians 3 proclaims to us very aggressively, "Watch out for them because your joy in the Lord must not be jeopardized." My translation of that—"Beware of anyone or anything that tries to divert you from just keeping your eyes upon Jesus!"

I have a confession to make. I have judged and have been critical of other people. I have made instant judgments based upon the appearance of an individual. In my "biblical" role of Sheriff of the Church, I have deduced motives based on one's church attendance or involvement in the church. I still get a pit in my stomach when I think of those times. Of this I repent. I've discovered that I wouldn't be so shocked at other people's sin (or if I were honest, of my own sin) if I didn't have such a high opinion of myself. Years ago I came across a cartoon portraying a game show entitled, "Is It Lawful?" The game show host was reading the questions while the panel of judges—three stern men in Pharisee garb—each sat before a pile of rocks, glaring at the contestant. As the judges prepared to throw their rocks, this poor guy sat there sweating bullets, awaiting the judgment of the panel. Lord, may this never be a picture of the congregation I serve.

There are a few things I've hopefully learned over the decades. I've learned that the right heart with the wrong ritual is far better than the wrong heart with the right ritual. I've learned that the righteousness of God is not a law-righteousness; it is a faith-righteousness. I've learned that religion is for people who want to stay out of Hell; Christianity is for people who have been there. And I've learned that when a person becomes a child of God, he comes under the influence of the law of love.

I love what Jim Cymbala said, "People aren't hungry for fancy sermons or organizational polish…They just want love." I've spent many hours pouring over and writing doctrinal position papers and what it always boils down to is a doctrinal position that is centered in and saturated with the love of Jesus. Why is it that our whole understanding of God is based on a quid pro quo of bartered love? Why is it that we buy into that crud that He will love us if we are good and moral and diligent? We try to live so that He will love us, rather than living because He has already loved us.

I came across a prayer I had written in my journal a number of years ago—"O Lord, don't give me strength to obey rules. Just keep changing my heart. May Your word not be a book of rules and regulations, but rather a living statement of Christ in me, the hope of glory. (Colossians 1:27)" And I ask myself, does my love and acceptance resound to the world as a powerful testimony of the reality of Jesus Christ in my life?

Why are we so quick to apply the law of sin and death to others? Part of the problem in the church today is that we live by a double-standard. We apply one set of rules to other people and another set to ourselves. Because of the spiritual arrogance that permeates many churches we really don't perceive ourselves as bad people. I love the bad news/good news premises of scripture. The bad news is that we are much worse off than we think. And the good news is God's love is a lot bigger than we think it is.

G.K. Chesterton was asked to write a letter to the London Times addressing this question, "What's Wrong with the World?" He responded by writing, "Dear sirs, I AM. Yours truly. G.K. Chesterton." I think that our ability to see ourselves as we really are makes us stiff in the presence of God. I have sensed a lot of stiffness in the church over the years. And you know what? I've learned something in my work with children.

3

Those lessons began in the course of my many short-term missions trips to Haiti. I've learned it's easier to hug a dirty kid than it is a stiff kid. I wonder which kid I am in the presence of God? Does our stiffness separate us from God? We need to come to the realization that the reason we feel guilty (if we allow ourselves to feel guilty) before the God of the universe is because we ARE guilty. He is holy and we are not. So we stiffen in His presence as well as in the presence of others. And the critical/bitter spirit within just continues to ferment as the years pass.

Paul says in Philippians 3:7—*Whatever was to my profit I now consider loss for the sake of Christ.* A lady was arguing with her pastor about the matter of faith and works. She said, "I think that getting to Heaven is like rowing a boat. One oar is faith and the other oar is works. If you use both, you'll get there; if you use only one, you go around in circles." There's only one thing wrong with that analogy. Nobody's going to Heaven in a rowboat. We go to Heaven IN CHRIST (period). There's only "one good work" that takes me, the sinner, to Heaven, and that is the finished work of Christ on the cross. And I don't care if you are a Bible-believing, fundamentalist, charismatic, restorationist, sanctified, holiness Christian. It profits you nothing apart from Jesus Christ. You can be circumcised, baptized, sanctified, homogenized and pasteurized and it profits you nothing apart from Jesus Christ!!

S. Lewis Johnson wrote an excellent article entitled, "The Paralysis of Legalism". I believe he puts his finger on the crux of the problem.

> "One of the most serious problems facing the orthodox Christian church today is the problem of legalism. One of the most serious problems facing the church of Paul's day was the problem of legalism. In every age it is the same. Legalism wrenches the joy of the Lord from the Christian believer, and with the joy of the Lord goes his

power for vital worship and vibrant service. Nothing is left but cramped, somber, dull, and listless profession. The truth is betrayed, and the glorious name of the Lord becomes a synonym for a gloomy kill-joy. The Christian under law is a miserable parody of the real thing."

It continues to blow me away when I see the issues that a large segment of the church is continuing to debate. Worse yet, they are trying to bind other Christians with these same legalistic issues. I got so agitated recently when a booklet came across my desk that told me because I enjoy and appreciate certain kinds of music that my spirit has been de-sensitized by the sensuality in my life. And that if I didn't have this battle with lust in my life I would have the RIGHT perspective on music and personally be offended by certain kinds of music. I struggle with anger when I see example after example of Christians putting together so-called biblical principles that come from horribly mutilated treatments of scripture and then use these "absolute" principles to bind other Christians and convince them to conform to certain practices, AND in the process rob them of the freedom and joy that they have in Christ Jesus.

Some would read the above words and question my commitment to biblical Christianity. That used to anger me. Now it just saddens me. "Commitment" is a fine word in most contexts. But as a religious word—a word to define my faith— it has, well, it has been pretty oppressive. It puts all the responsibility for my relationship with God on my shoulders. And that's just too great a burden for me, or anyone, to bear. If I am to be a "committed" Christian then I am consistent, regular, disciplined, strong-willed…That doesn't sound much like biblical Christianity; it sounds more like a diet. I wish I had a dollar for every time over the past 40 years I've been asked if I were committed. Commitment is a discipline; characterized by very hard work, and there's nothing wrong with that. But in my dictionary I discovered the word, "hunger"; and my soul begins to tingle. My faith isn't so much a discipline as it is a hunger. I had been hungry for God from the very beginning. I wanted to hang around God, to know God. However when I went to Bible college, much of the teaching I received collided with those leanings. I was full of unnamed longings for God, but I was told to be cautious and not become too emotion-oriented in my walk with God. I was told that what was relevant was my "commitment"—to Bible reading and prayer and witnessing and stuff. Nothing wrong with any of these, I practice them all. But these were all things that had to do with God. They were never enough in and of themselves. They were on the periphery of God. How many times do we suppress our hunger for God, instead of appreciating and cultivating it? A hunger for God is a gift, a sign of the Holy Spirit working, an assurance that God is alive in my heart. Hunger for God is the fertilizer in which commitments grow; the foundation upon which commitments are made.

A man was once asked, "Why is your church so different?" And he responded, "Our leadership has given us the permission to be free." I guess that's why I just love that song we've been singing in our church the last couple of years—"I AM FREE."

> "Through You the blind will see; through You the mute will sing;
> Through You the dead will rise; through You all hearts will praise;
> Through You the darkness flees; Through You my heart screams 'I am free!'
> I am free to run – I am free to dance – I am free to live for You; I am free, I am free."
> (Written by John Egan. c 2004 Vertical Group Worship Songs)

May people always look at the church I serve and say, "O yeah. I know about that church. They give each other the permission to be free." I wonder where the ridiculous idea originated that every single moment in life must be grim and sober. Why can't we break the thick and brittle mold of predictability or the bondage of tunnel vision? I refuse to live the rest of my years playing one note on one instrument in one room. May I find pleasure in the symphony of sounds and sights and smells all around me. May I step into an anxiety and tension-free existence where I can feel the wind and smell the wildflowers and hug my wife and giggle with my grandkids and laugh until I'm hoarse. I think it's all about freedom. That's it plain and simple. And the bottom line—it's about GRACE. I think I'll give myself permission to appreciate God's grace and freedom, instead of worrying about who might say what!

When a person becomes a child of God, he comes under the influence of the law of love. When I threaten to become cold in my ministry (which is almost every time I start focusing on law) and my heart is not filled with amazement at the love of God; when the Lord's Supper becomes rather passé; it is then that I begin to review the sins of my past life and enter into that broken spirit the Bible talks about (Psalm 51:17). And I am ready to preach once more. And more often than not, I am ready to preach the love of God. For the last three years one of my daily prayers has been to "allow Christ's love to be experienced by those who are around me." Praying that prayer every day keeps that goal before me constantly. "Lord, may those around me sense and see His love in me."

Renowned psychologist, Carl Jung wrote, "I only wish the Christians of today could see for once that what many of them stand for is not Christianity at all, but rather a God-awful legalistic religion from which Jesus Christ Himself tried to free them." Let me tell you something about that freedom and that love. Your grade has already been given to you when you

7

come into Jesus Christ. You have already received your report card. It happened on the cross and you got an "A". When we give others the permission to be free in Christ, it means we not only realize that we have received an unearned "A", but we are willing to give our brothers and sisters in Jesus an unearned "A" as well.

So, what have I concluded about Love vs. law?

1. When I focus on law, I become critical in spirit

2. A right heart takes precedent over right ritual

3. My faith is driven by a hunger for God

4. My freedom in Jesus is what enables me to make a difference

My love letter to Jesus (taken from my journals)

"My Jesus I love Thee. I love You, Lord because you first loved me (1 John 4:19). I have never figured out why You do, but I know that You do. Thank You for loving me, in spite of me (my attitudes, my negativity, my sin, my selfishness, and I could go on and on). Amazing love, how can it be................"

Chapter Two – Truth Over Common Sense

There will be those who will read the first chapter of this book and question my "commitment" to the Lordship of Christ and accuse me of being a proponent of "easy believism." The Lord taught me some time ago that BALANCE is an important key to my life and my ministry, so I would guess this ingrained truth compels me to follow the "love chapter" with a chapter about truth, as if they were separate entities. (Eph. 4:15)

Bob Russell, former senior pastor of Southeast Christian Church in Louisville shared a prayer with me years ago. It's a prayer that is taped in the flyleaf of his Bible. After receiving it, I also taped it in my Bible. It's still there today. This prayer is a classic.

> "Before I break the bread of life, Lord, break me! Wash from my heart and lips the iniquity there. I want to preach, yes, hemorrhage under the divine anointing. God, strip me of all pride, all cleverness, all showmanship. Let Christ be exalted, the Cross be central, and the Plea be with passion. May my eyes never be dry. Just now, Lord, take me out of myself, usurp anything I've planned to say when it's in the way of Your message. Here I am, Lord. I'm Your vessel! Amen."

Does my congregation realize that I am preaching the gospel of Jesus Christ solely and simply because I happen to believe that it is true? Our walk with God must be saturated in the truth of His Word. Jesus said in John 4 that we are to worship in spirit and in truth. Our greatest worship is to open God's Word and allow the Spirit to touch our hearts with it (and change our lives). Yes, the fruit must be produced. My vision of God is not an ecstasy or a dream, but an understanding of what God wants. I admit that I don't always know what that is; but growing understanding has to come from His Word. It is His Word that is to instruct me and fill me and guide me. In the last chapter I talked about my love relationship with God. Reading, applying and obeying God's Word are keys which unlock that love relationship with Him. I have come to firmly believe the church is not called to success, at least the kind of the success defined for us by many church growth consultants. The church is called to deliver God's truth and to BE truth for the praise of His glory. The church must stand for the glory of God and for what God can do through us to make a difference in our culture, rather than a socialistic institution under the patronage of God.

It seems we aren't having any trouble getting people to believe today. Everybody believes (something). But I wonder sometimes how many in the church are truly changed. I listen carefully to what our churches proclaim (from pulpit, radio, TV) and I think, no wonder everyone "believes." It can be such an easy sell. And I've decided that maybe my ministry needs to zero in on less "answers" for everything and more "questions" for my flock. Questions like, "What are you doing in ministry today that you can only accomplish through the power of God?" That's just one question out of, oh, maybe a thousand.

I've often said that ministry was a lot more fun when I knew everything. An interesting phenomenon in my life in recent years is the discovery that the older I get, the more questions I have. There are many things I do not understand. I don't understand why children die or are abused. I get upset when people start talking about guardian angels and I wonder what that kid's angel was doing when he was beaten and molested. Years ago a mentor of mine counseled me, "Rick, never let a lack of understanding come between your heart and your Lord." There may be many things that challenge my understanding, but they must never come in between my heart and God.

I had always heard that common sense was a commodity that was to be sought after. Not that I'm anti-common sense, but I've come to the conclusion that common sense is not always the golden egg it's cracked up to be (no pun intended). There are spiritual truths that sometimes defy common sense. There are very clear teachings in scripture that are diametrically opposed to common sense. Grace and forgiveness and the whole doctrine of salvation by faith in Christ alone (which I believe and embrace heart and soul) make no sense empirically. Let me give you two quotations from Martin Luther. The first one is not very spiritual. The second is far more acceptable in church. The first thing he said was, "It's better to be drunk than sad." That was spoken, I suspect, in jest. But then again, maybe not. There are some things Luther said that I wouldn't quote to you in this book. The second quotation, however, is a bit more proper. He said, "Remorse before Calvary is of God; remorse after you have been there is of the devil." Luther struggled with depression and remorse all of his life and it should be no surprise that he would speak often of those subjects.

Have you ever wondered why Paul talked so much about grace and forgiveness and about the doctrine of salvation by faith in Christ alone? In 1 Timothy 1:15, Paul says, *This is a faithful saying and worthy of all acceptance, that Christ Jesus came into the world to save sinners, of whom I am chief.* Paul became the great teacher of grace for one simple reason; he needed grace and forgiveness so desperately. Let me give you a principle that I wish I would have comprehended early in my ministry. The principle is this—great truth grows in the soil of great need!! Without the need, there would be very little reception to the important truth of the gospel. That means that some of us have gotten it backwards. We think that those who have no need, who have everything right, and who walk perfectly with Christ are to be the teachers and preachers and leaders, when in fact just the opposite is true. I think that the preachers and teachers who have risen out of the muck of greatest need become the most dynamic leaders. The whole concept of grace makes absolutely no sense to me when I turn on the logic and common sense computer in my brain. I jubilantly say with Paul, *thank God for saving me through Jesus Christ our Lord* (Romans 7:25) and *There is now no condemnation for those who are in Christ Jesus* (Romans 8:1). I don't comprehend it all, but I refuse to allow my lack of understanding to come between my heart and my Lord.

Life is hard and unfair and unpredictable. It's filled with disappointments. You will not find the word "fair" in your concordance. We as Christians are not exempt from problems or suffering. Our promise from God is that our suffering will not be in vain. We humans tend to believe our hardships are all about us. How arrogant!! As Christians, it is never about us…God is in control. He will always and ultimately have His way. I remember after 9-11, network news reported that "we don't know who the enemy is."

No kidding! We don't have a clue. We certainly haven't figured out who the enemy of our soul is. Our problem is that either we don't comprehend that being separated from God IS our problem, or we just don't care. It's time that the church realizes "this world is not my home; I'm just a-passin through." We need to LIVE like it—not in fear, but in divine confidence. Watchman Nee (Chinese preacher and author of approximately 55 books), says it well. "To hold on to the plough; while wiping our tears; this is Christianity." In other words, keep on keeping on while we are daily about the business of loving God and loving others. What a great biblical definition of the Christian walk. Nee worked feverishly to establish local assemblies throughout China. In 1949 he was imprisoned for his faith by the Chinese government and remained in prison until his death twenty years later.

It is an ongoing struggle for me. But I continue to learn and relearn the following principles when it comes to truth over common sense.

1. To honor the marriage of love AND truth

2. Everybody believes something…It DOES matter what you believe

3. Never let a lack of understanding come between your heart and your Lord

4. Great truth grows in the soil of great need

What do you delight in? Some days my greatest delight is a good steak. Other days it is my grandkids. Sometimes I argue with God's Word, but how often do I delight in it? Phillip Yancey said, "All our doubts about God and suffering should be filtered through what we know about Jesus Christ." That is to be my focus; NOT my circumstances. God is faithful even when I am not. He says to me, "Get ready Jones to be amazed." We are never, never without hope. God is not calling us to be "Christian". He is calling us to be a holy people; to make a difference in our culture. Don't demand things from God ("Gotta be my way; my agenda"). He knows what He's doing. God says, "Trust Me; your future is in My hands." And you know what? I truly believe it; but it flies in the face of every bit of common sense I know.

Chapter Three – Child-likeness Over Arrogant Adulthood

Late one evening, premier American evangelist of the 1880s, Dwight L. Moody, arrived home from speaking at a meeting. Emma, his wife, was already asleep. As her exhausted husband climbed into bed, she rolled over and murmured, "So how did it go tonight?" "Pretty well," he replied. "Two and one-half converts to Jesus." His wife lay silently for a moment pondering this response, then finally smiled, "That's sweet," she replied. "How old was the child?" "No," said Moody. "It was two children and one adult. The children have their whole lives in front of them. The adult's life is already half-gone."

Most of us, me included, would have had the same mental image as Emma Moody—Two and a half converts—Two adults standing there in that service with a little child next to them. If that's what you envisioned, don't feel bad. Most do. It's a very natural pattern of thinking. But we need to change our natural pattern of thinking—the world today calls that a paradigm shift—and our world needs that kind of paradigm shift.

One of my mentors said to me years ago, "We have made ourselves very complicated." Yes we have. At the beginning of each year I make a list of prayer goals for myself (usually 5 or 6). One of my prayer goals the last couple of years has been, "Lord, cultivate the kid in me." Lizatte Woodworth Reese, in her writings proclaims, "Lord, I am a child again; joy holds me fast." Oswald Chambers says, "A child's life ought to be a child's life—full of simplicity." I have learned through the years that I gain a fresh perspective when I choose to look at life through the eyes of a child. The more time I spend with children (including my own precious grandchildren) the easier this becomes. The most effective way to keep in touch with my own childlike spirit is simply to spend time with little people. One of my responsibilities at our church has been oversight and teaching in our elementary ministries. On one recent Sunday morning we were in the midst of a teaching on "things that God hates". The kids were asked to think of things that He hates and hands went up all over the auditorium. We received great comments such as "the devil," "sin," "drugs," etc. But the entire core of adults in the room broke up when one 4th grader with a smile on his face said, "Green beans." I still laugh when I think about it.

I don't want to over-romanticize childhood or suggest that being child-like is an infallible route to happiness. But how much more meaningful will our lives be if we manage to acquire the virtues and advantages of maturity without sacrificing the child-like qualities that keep us closer to the true joy of the Lord?

"Kids are so neat! Sometimes they are bundles of energy, gift-wrapped in hand-me-downs. At other times they're pajama-clad packages of sleepy sweetness. ALWAYS they are a miracle!! I love the way they chase butterflies and the attention they give to mud puddles and raindrops on the window. I envy their freedom from clocks and calendars and their immunity to pressure. Oh, they have their moments; skinned knees and nap times, but they recover quickly. They don't nurse their disappointments or make a career of holding grudges. Kids are so neat. Lord, let me be converted and become as a little child. Let me know the sheer joy of being alive, and the pure pleasure of living one day at a time, fully savoring each solitary moment. Free me from past disappointments and from the little hurts I've so carefully kept. Restore to me a childlike anticipation for life, a sense of wonder which makes each new day and my life truly abundant."

(Personal Journal – May 5, 1988)

It's been said that wonder is an encounter with the reality of God that brings awe to the heart. I don't think we cultivate or nurture this wondering spirit enough—this gift from the Holy Spirit. It is the "child spirit." Are we like a child; always wide awake with wonder? Wonder is where it all begins. All of us have our hidden "Narnia" (thank you, C.S. Lewis). All of us can go back into time in our lives when dreams of a life fulfilled with wonder throbbed in our souls. And then we abruptly hit the ground as we touch down on the mundane. Idealism can die with knowledge. Analysis can be the death knell of mystery. Reality, many times, undercuts wonder. Where did we ever get the idea that we are entitled to all of the answers to all of the mysteries concerning our faith? No, you certainly do not have to, and no one should expect you to assassinate your brain to be a Christian; but when did our walk with God become an empirical test tube experience? One great preacher of yesterday was asked about the "success" of his ministry. He replied, "I've never lost the wonder!"

Have you ever listened (I mean really listened) to a child pray? Those who are seniors in the school of prayer aren't usually those who pray the best prayers. Those who understand all of the doctrinal truths about prayer or have spent a lifetime in monasteries are not always the deepest pray-ers. Those who have "God's ear" are often the children as well as those who have learned to "grow down" and become childlike.

I am learning that becoming more childlike in my prayers is a primary requirement for effective prayer. Effective praying seems to have a lack of sophistication and slickness. Part of my childlikeness is getting serious about not being so serious. I guess that's why I fell in love with that chorus, *Abba Father*. I still tear up when I sing those lyrics to myself.

Abba Father
My Defender
You are Holy
And I surrender
For in my weakness
You protect me
When my heart strays
You Correct me

I cry Abba Father -
I love you, Daddy
Abba Father...
I love you, I love you
I cry Abba Father -
I love you, Daddy
Abba Father..
I love you I love you
Daddy

Will Campbell writes that addressing God as "Dear Abba," is the first tentative and informal sound made at the baby's first taste of cereal—"Abababab". When the disciples asked Jesus to teach them to pray He began by saying, "Our Father". Campbell says, "Father (Abba) is family. He is our Daddy; our Papa." And I am beginning to realize how much my Father really wants to spend time with me. I am practicing backing away from my more adult images and inhibitions and getting more and more familiar with my heavenly Papa. I am learning that childlikeness is a matter of trust, that He really is in control and I can believe Him when He says, "Don't be afraid." And I am slowly learning to trust, even when I am hurting. Know what? Children don't bring any power to the throne of God. Being childlike is to recognize how powerless I am. Even when I achieve inner peace for a time, I still have that deep sense of my own inadequacy and dependence, and I have to admit my inability to make my power or strength or love any greater.

I have been criticized in the past for being too naïve or idealistic. I have sometimes questioned myself in this. But I am learning that a growing childlikeness will make me even more idealistic, yes, sometimes even more naïve, even sometimes bordering upon presumption. Maybe we in church leadership need more of that; to not take ourselves so seriously; to lighten up a bit. I have learned that my relationship with the Lord is serious, but not a sour or gloomy thing.

I have to confess! I am a Christmas junkie!! I have always been a Christmas junkie. I start Christmas shopping the day after Thanksgiving and begin watching Christmas movies the same day. I have our tree up and outside decorations hung the first week of December and I nag my wife to get the rest of the house decorations up ASAP. I find myself getting more and more excited as Christmas draws near. I know that I'm 64 years old. Lord, cultivate the kid in me!! I am very fortunate to have married a bride who has helped to keep the "magic" alive in me. Remember Lucy, the youngest child in *The Lion, The Witch, and the Wardrobe?* Her faith is unwavering. Even when everyone else tells her that what she believes is false; she forcefully declares her undying convictions! Frederick Beuchner writes, "When Jesus is asked who is the greatest in the Kingdom, He reaches into the crowd and pulls a child with a cheek full of bubble gum and eyes full of whatever a child's eyes are full of and says that unless you are willing to become like that, don't bother asking?" From Jesus' perspective it takes the humility and wonder and faith of a child to grasp what the Kingdom is all about—childlike faith. And those of us who think we are too grown up or cool for all that simple faith business are missing the mark. I see so many copping an attitude of cool and hoping it passes for smart. I keep asking the question to any who will listen, "What will it take for you to be a kid again?

And that reminds me that another sign of childlikeness is a growing and irrepressible joy in me. The closer I move to His throne, the less serious a lot of other stuff becomes. Sometimes people of faith are wary of too much laughter, often because we think it's childish. My dear wife has taught me the great lessons of Proverbs 15:13; 15—*A happy heart makes the face cheerful...the cheerful heart has a continual feast.* She has lived that truth for years and taught it to me. It is CHILDLIKE to laugh from your belly.

It is childlike to trust so much that you slip your hand into your Father's and skip down the sidewalk. Some Christians spend time and effort reading too much into things or reading "between the lines". Lighten up. Enjoy your life in the Lord. There is a joy in resting in the One who is in charge. When we are in a relationship with God there is a childlike joy in knowing that we are accepted and cherished no matter what. Children always have a way about them and will say what's on their minds. Why don't we do that with God? Do we think He doesn't know how we feel? Do we think He somehow doesn't really get it? One of the most important things I have discovered about my time alone with God is that I can say things to God that I could never say any other place, because no one would understand.

My daughter Becky overheard her youngest daughter, Grace, say a word that wasn't used in their home. She promptly let her know that she was not to use that word again. After Becky left the room, Grace said to her older sister, Chloe, "Guess what; I'm still saying it in my head." Isn't that the spirit of rebellion that's a part of all of us? My heavenly Father will always love and accept me no matter what I say to Him (even if it's just in my head).

And that makes me think about another example of a childlike spirit. I remember years ago my daughter, Christine, coming home with a typical 9 year old remark, "I'll never speak to Patty again!" She was very angry with Patty (her friend). Now she, being a restrained "civilized" young lady, refrained from scratching out Patty's eyes. Instead she did the more civilized thing: she refused to speak. To act as if another does not exist is a more hostile act than to slap their face. In slapping a person (and I certainly don't advocate that action) one at least acknowledges their presence. The silent treatment is an extremely powerful weapon of aggression. With God, we are seemingly unable to hurt Him in any other way except by our silence. This silence is our "weapon of revenge" for the bad stuff He has allowed to happen to us. Like my daughter, we'll show Him; we just won't speak to Him. Note that David never went that route. Even when he was angry with God or hurt or confused, he talked to the Lord; he let it all hang out. Ever yell at God? David did. Guess what? GOD CAN HANDLE IT!! He knows more about what's going on inside of us that we do. My silent treatment with God has NEVER solved anything. He KNOWS when I'm "saying it in my head."

Childlikeness is telling God where it hurts. I don't want to "tip-toe through the tulips" with Jesus. I want to be painfully honest with Him. And I want to learn from Him and grow in Him. I have so many questions. But somehow the questions begin to fade when I am spending time with my Father. Jesus reserved His greatest anger for arrogance and judgmentalism. But the children (and the prostitutes and the sinners)—He just loved on them!!

So, what have I learned about this childlike spirit?

1. Choose to look at life through the eyes of a child

2. Never lose the wonder!

3. Keep "growing down" and practice being childlike in praying, in trust, and in honesty with God.

Have you ever watched a child struggle with a task such as tying his shoe? I remember one of my daughters crying in frustration, "Daddy, I try and I try and I can't do it." St. Augustine said, "Understanding is the reward of faith; therefore seek not to understand that you may believe; but rather believe that you may understand." In other words, the childlike spirit is all about trust. I try; I fail! I trust; I succeed! I love it!!

> John Greenleaf Whittier wrote, "All the windows of my heart I open to the day. Yes, Lord; this day!! Father, keep phoniness away from my spirit and my countenance. Fill me with authenticity. Make me real; especially in my walk with You."

Cultivate the kid in me.

Chapter Four – People Over Programs

I was only in my early twenties when my first daughter was born. Had I known then what I know now, I would have been terrified. I had no idea that my relationship with Christine would shape her relationship with her heavenly Father; that she would unconsciously attribute to God the Father, the strengths and weaknesses she saw in me. Nor did I realize that my words would forever mold her self-image, giving her confidence to follow her dreams or lock her into a prison of inferiority. I had no idea how important the gift of my presence would be, or how much she would depend upon my counsel and guidance. On that day when she entered into the world (January 2, 1968) I was too naïve to realize that I was embarking on the most important ministry of my life; and that if I failed as a father, all of my other accomplishments and achievements would somehow be diminished.

Today my eldest lives in Chicago with her husband, three children and her two cats. She recently completed her nursing education and works in a large hospital in the suburbs. I couldn't be more proud. Years ago, she wrote a piece of verse that I have saved. She is a good writer in her own right. I read it periodically:

> "self portrait of me
> they all think they know the girl they see in me
> but very few will find who i am honestly
> i come across strong but i'm so very weak

> i know everything but answers i seek
> look on the outside confidence soars
> look on the inside my insecurity pours
> i wear my heart for all to see
> can't hide or fake it though i try endlessly
> i have a passion for life i carry an inner joy
> though some try to steal it as if it were a toy
> most don't get me they don't comprehend
> that most of it's a show it's all pretend
> but some will find my special place
> touching my soul bring smiles to my face
> if you're one of the few who know the real me
> count yourself blessed i allowed you to see"

I read those words when I need to be reminded of what my ministry is all about. The church is called to be the church. And when the church is truly the church, every member of the body is treated as an individual. What is more important than people? Aren't God's people to be cherished and not simply to be counted? I am not a number. I am a precious soul for whom Jesus died. We are so much more than lines on a graph or a set of demographic statistics. We are a people who laugh and cry, have pain and joy, and have a deep, deep need to know that God values us for who we are.

The mission statement of our church over the last number of years is based upon the words of Jesus in Matthew 22—TO LOVE GOD AND LOVE OTHERS. I don't see a lot about technique or programming in the New Testament. Unless we are particularly heroic or saintly persons (Guess what? I'm not!), each of us needs intimate relationships with other people who love and seek and trust in simple ways. Such relationships become enormously supportive to us. The rigorous demands of that kind of interaction: the gift of oneself, one's time, one's preferences, the nakedness and honesty toward each other, are beyond the price many are willing to pay. But the longer I am here, the more and more I am convinced it is vital to pay that price. Anyone who has been graced (as I have) with a true love relationship knows the cost and knows the worth of that relationship. Methods and systems and principles are all fine, but I must never forget that my first priority is to love my precious Father in heaven; and then to love others.

In the Fall of 2006 I was preparing to teach our teen group. As I studied I was reminded of an experience many years ago when I served as a juvenile probation officer in Northern Michigan. I was assigned a 13 year old boy in my caseload, who, among other things had a drug problem. He had been arrested with a friend for extensively vandalizing a summer residence. Both boys were high. Because of his home situation (and other problems) he had a very poor concept of how God viewed him. I'll call him "Charlie;" (the name has been changed to protect the guilty). I thought about Charlie as I prepared to share with our teens. I was reading Psalm 17:8—*Guard me, O Lord, as the apple of your eye; hide me in the shadow of your wings.* I'm happy to say that Charlie is married today with kids of his own, a good career and a wonderful walk with the Lord. As his life was beginning to turn around (probably about his sophomore year) he wrote a piece of verse that deeply touched my heart. The closing lines of his writing was something he had heard (I think it originally came from a high school student in central Indiana). His words still find a place in my heart today—"I'm me; I'm good; cause God don't make no junk."

I have learned (sometimes through difficult experience) that my ministry is not about the philosophy I adopt or the words I use in a sermon. My ministry is to be centered in identifying myself with God's interests in other people!! We use a phrase in our church often—"It's not about me." That's very true. But then we go on to say, "It's about Him." That is also true. But if it is truly "about Him", God says that it is also to be about "others." In other words, if my ministry is about Him; it must be about YOU. As confessed in the previous chapter, I am a big fan of Christmas. And I am also a huge fan of dear Mother Teresa. I love her words—"It's Christmas time every time you let God love others through you. Yes, it's Christmas every time you smile at your brother and offer him your hand."

A number of years ago, my youngest daughter, Becky was convicted to take a year off of college to go to Haiti and teach school. She taught second graders in the northern coastal city of Port-au-Paix. I gave her a letter the day she left. I believe that the content of that letter reveals the heart and soul of what I am inadequately trying to convey in this chapter.

"Dear Becky,

It's been a while since I've told you what a special person you are. God has given you the gift of joy and self-confidence. I think you have tremendous people skills and a real talent for speaking and drama (and of course, music). Never forget, though, that when God gives a person special gifts, He also gives them special responsibilities. Always remember:

1) Attitude is everything—It is the one thing no one can take from you—the freedom to choose how you are going to feel or react about any situation.

2) Relationships are the most important things in life…Always be careful to use things and love people.

3) Don't be afraid to fail…Great things are rarely achieved on the first try.

4) God's will is not inhibiting…It frees you to fulfill your highest potential, while enjoying the most meaningful life possible.

5) If you sin, God always stands ready to forgive.

6) True joy is found in striving for God-given goals, even more than obtaining them; so dare to dream big dreams, dare to attempt great things for God.

One last thing—Always remember how much your Mom and I love you. There is nothing you can do (or not do), no success or achievement (or failure) which will ever make us love you more or less. We love you, not because of what you do, but because of who you are.

Love, Dad"

Perhaps the summary of this letter is a parent giving a daughter the permission to be free. I wonder if we treat each other that way in the body of Christ. Just knowing that someone else is struggling, as you are, in their walk with the Lord is a great encouragement. When another knows and cares about what you do, then we pay much more attention to what we're doing. Many times it isn't the "outside" of a person that draws you to him/her. Do you love the spirit of your brother, or do you just love the outside of him? If you penetrate to that inner soul and truly love it—not some imaginary illusion you've concocted about him—but his own true soul, and love it, then he is really and truly a brother. In that kind of relationship, the true strength given to your friend by God becomes his joy. Then it's not just a "buddy" thing; it's a God-thing!! And it is this God-thing that makes the difference. In all of my relationships, it's not that I feel I'm nothing. Rather I believe that I am nothing without God. HE is the difference in all of my relationships. HE makes the difference in how I view and value and treat others.

Dietrich Bonhoeffer in his writing, *Life Together,* said, "A Christian fellowship lives and exists by the intercession of its members for one another, or it collapses. What a truth. I can no longer hate or have bad feelings toward a brother for whom I pray, no matter what I think he has done to me or how much I disagree with him. When I pray for him (and Jesus says I must pray for him) his face is transformed before me (in intercession) into the countenance of a brother for whom Christ died, the face of a forgiven sinner. There is no dislike, no personal tension, no estrangement that cannot be overcome by intercession as far as our side is concerned. Intercession for each other is a purifying bath into which the individual and the fellowship must enter every day."

How does this happen? Intercession means no more than to bring your brother (or sister) into the presence of God, to see him under the cross of Jesus as a poor human being and sinner in need of grace. And then everything in him that turns me off falls away. And get this: Intercession means to grant our brother the same right we have received, namely, to stand before Christ and share in His mercy. Know what? Call it intercessory relationship or whatever you desire; it has absolutely nothing to do with programming or technique or philosophy of ministry or methodology. Thank God!!

People over programs…OH YES!! Summary? …

1. My ministry is to be centered in identifying myself with God's interests in other people

2. We need to give each other permission to be free

3. Christ in me makes the difference in how I view and value and treat others

"It is great to do the Lord's work...But the greatest work is to do the Lord's will...While we glimpse the glory of God in Jesus...The world needs to glimpse the glory of Jesus in us." (Ancient writer)

Chapter Five – Master Over Ministry

"Lord, it's Rick."

"I know."

I'm having trouble with this sermon."

"I know."

"You know, Lord, it's getting late and I've got this deadline coming up soon."

"I know."

"I'm uncomfortable with what I've done so far on this sermon."

"I know. Your discomfort is from Me. I gave it to you so that you would come to Me."

""Lord, help me to discover some important things about praying."

"OK."

"How can I do that?"

"How about starting to pray?"

"Lord, You are wonderful and incredible!"

"I know."

(Personal journal – January 6, 2003 –

Adapted from a message by Steve Brown)

No one is indispensable in the Kingdom. No one ever has been. Were there ever any great men born in LaPorte County? No, they were all babies.

I suspect that God does whatever He wants, and for some reason He has never checked with me about hardly anything. There have been many times in my ministry when I have said, "O God, I can't do this." And God says, "Good. You're finally where I want you to be." I am still learning to make my choices reflect the priorities I say I have. God asks, "Will you finally let Me make a way for you?" How many times has my arrogant and stubborn spirit told God what I want Him to do in my life and ministry and how I want Him to accomplish it?

I received a letter from a former mentor some years ago. It read, "Remember, my friend, don't take yourself too seriously. This is about God's Spirit working in the lives of people to draw them nearer to Jesus; not to you. We are called to serve them. Preach the Word faithfully, and then disappear into the background so that God will get the praise." Yes!! There is no room for personal vanity when the standard that is to be seen is the Lord Himself. I've preached it again and again over the years—Our purpose as the church is to glorify God—to bring all glory and honor to Him. And this has brought a key question to my attention repeatedly—"Who will truly be the authority in my life?" The test of every spiritual impulse is, "Does it make Jesus Christ Lord of all?" Our ministry is evaluated in God's sight by whether or not we clear the way for people to see Jesus. A man with the vision of God is not devoted to a cause or to any particular issue; he is devoted to the Lord Himself. Oswald Chambers said, "Your duty in service and ministry is to see that there is nothing between Jesus and yourself."

> "Today I am totally focusing on Jesus. He is all that matters…HE IS ALL!! What about the small stuff, the peripheral areas? Who cares? Christ is my focus."

(Personal journal – July 19, 1991)

The older I become the less I worry about what people think and the more I concern myself with what God thinks. When I get His "green light", I confess my weakness and my apprehension, then I move in that direction, and He and I have the time of our lives. But invariably there will be those who do not understand His working in me. I have committed not to take my cues from those who frown back at me (as some have done, many times). I mean, what do they know about my life or the Lord's working in my life anyway? I have come to realize that the life of ministry is not so much "progress" as it is "process". It is not a continuous climb upward as much as it is continuous. It is not the victories that matter so much as the keeping on after the defeats. The longer my life of faith goes on, the less I care about what God is doing and the more I want to know God. Spirituality, after all, is intimacy with Him. In my journey with Him I have been called to that intimacy. That was and is the heart of my "calling" to be a pastor.

And yet, there have been many times that I have encountered that "deer-in-the-headlights" stare from young men when I have asked them about their calling. I actually had one guy say to me, "I attended a class on preaching at a Bible college and I thought to myself, 'I can do that'; and if it doesn't work out, I can always go into photography." I believe that a preacher/pastor is one who has realized the call of God and is determined to use his every energy to proclaim God's truth. The pastoral ministry is NOT just another job. Questionable ministries many times have externals that seem right, but internally they are far from God. My desire is to be as a musician who does not heed the approval of the audience. Rather it is to catch the look of approval from my Master. Through the years I've developed a personal motto for my ministry—"Whenever I think I am adequate to be faithful in my own strength, I am in trouble." The call to preach is not because I have a special gift, or because Jesus has sanctified me in some special, mysterious manner. The call is that I have had a glimpse of the cross and life can never be the same again.

One of the most difficult times in my ministry was the spring and summer of 1978. I had been serving as youth pastor in a downtown Michigan City, Indiana congregation for seven years. I was very sure that God was preparing me for change but was confused as to what that meant. It was at this time that a small group within the congregation was praying about starting a new church work in LaPorte County. I immediately became excited about that potential, but was uncertain that my enthusiasm was of the Lord. By June, I knew that I was to terminate my present ministry, but I was sure of nothing beyond that.

To add to the confusion, by mid-June, I received five different offers from churches in the Midwest. The confusion intensified. Where was I to go? Where did God want me? It was during this time that I developed a kind of check list of questions to ask myself daily as I prayed for God's specific direction. I still have this list taped inside of my Bible.

1. Will this decision enable me to grow in grace?
2. Is it God's best for my life?
3. Is it in keeping with the life and message of Jesus?
4. Can I do this and still seek first His kingdom and righteousness?
5. Does it will the ultimate good for me?
6. Is it part of the long-range goals the Lord has already revealed to me?
7. Am I really exhibiting "raw trust" in my Lord?

I prayed through these questions each day and then simply asked the Lord to start closing doors in front of me. By the second week of July, every door was slammed shut except a call to new church work in LaPorte Country. Things really started moving quickly. On August 6, 1978 Countryside Christian Church was born with 54 charter members. I remember sharing with that infant church in our first few weeks a quote from Oswald Chambers, "Is my confidence now placed in God Himself, and not in His blessings? If I am depending upon anything but Him, I will never know when He is gone." With that confidence in our sovereign Lord we have seen that little body of people grow to over a thousand weekly. I've been asked by many, "What is the secret of your success?" I would hope never to be so arrogant as to even try to answer that question. But I do know that confidence in the Lord and the humble, sacrificial spirits in many individuals over the years have been a part of it.

> "Remember that your fruit is always to be stored up for Jesus; only that fruit in which Jesus alone is glorified and we take no credit. Let my fruit be only for my Lord and not for the world." (Personal journal – October 1, 1996)

Master over ministry!! I have labored long and hard to convey to my flock that kind of confidence and humility and sacrifice. How many in our culture today (including the church) have become experts at seeing to it that we do our ministry with as little inconvenience as possible? I have asked our congregation many times, "How much has your ministry cost you? What price have you paid?" The issue isn't how much you gave away; the issue is how much did you keep for yourself. We have a job to do. We have all been called to make a difference. If you don't have enough time to do ministry then you need to reorganize your time priorities. I am done apologizing for asking God's people to pay the price.

> "Lord, help me to focus today on God stuff and not church stuff. May I stop reading books about the emerging church for a while and simply honor the discipline of silence and

wait upon You. I will not try to direct the Spirit, but rather be guided by Him."

(Personal journal – February 13, 2005)

There have been many crossroads for me in my 29 years as senior pastor at Countryside.

I would regress and forget that it wasn't "my" ministry; but rather it was "His" ministry. Periodically He would have to remind me that my identity wasn't found in Countryside Christian Church. My identity was to be found in Him. I would forget that Christian "work" can sometimes be a means of evading my concentration on Jesus Christ. I would learn and relearn the principle that if I take on the work of God and get out of touch with Him, the sense of responsibility becomes overwhelmingly crushing. I needed (still do sometimes) to practice daily walking with my burdens upon Him. Those lessons are still being learned.

Master over ministry became so vivid to me once again when God began placing in my spirit the need to step down as senior pastor at Countryside. I was only 60 when that nudging began. I still have a lot of good years left. Why now? But God was relentless in leading me to this decision. "It's time for a change," He would impress upon me. And in the summer of 2005 I was ready. I was part of a short-term missions trip to Mexico, a number of us working alongside of our missionaries, Darren and Judith Saldebuhere. During that week the Lord and I had some intense conversations regarding "my" ministry. I was pushing 62 years of age. I remember a teen saying to me, "You really look younger, from a distance." I knew of very few men who continued to do well leading a church this size after the age of 60. I was aware of some who made futile attempts to ride their past reputation into the future, but they did not finish strong. God convinced me that week in Mexico that it was His will and His timing for me to step down. The following week, I met with our eldership and shared with them that I would be stepping down in a year or so and they needed to start praying for my replacement. The next year was extremely difficult as I daily wrestled with letting go of "my" ministry. I could almost feel the void even before I stepped down. But God was at work filling that void before it was reality. Before God called me to ministry, I was set on going into elementary education in the public school system. The last couple of years of my senior pastorate, God was preparing me for new ministry. I had begun volunteering in a fourth grade class one afternoon a week. That experience led to my being approached to secure a state substitute teacher's license. Also, during this time the eldership at Countryside asked me to pray about leading the children's ministry. I served in that capacity for almost two years.

Today, three years after stepping down as senior pastor, I come to another leg in my journey. I resigned this summer as part-time children's pastor at Countryside and will devote my full time to teaching in the public school system, private tutoring and pastoral counseling.

What have my ministry experiences taught me about Master over ministry?

1. It's NEVER "my" ministry
2. Jesus is all that matters
3. Many times Christian "work" can take my eyes off Jesus
4. The call to ministry is from God…Answering His call brings peace

Chapter Six – Quietness Over Busyness

"Let my body be a servant of my spirit and both my body and spirit be servants of Jesus, doing all things for God's glory." (Jeremy Taylor)

> "I think of rest a lot lately, Lord. When I weary, when I feel I must have rest and retreat, help me to constantly recognize that my rest and refreshment is in You. Often I need to be stopped (*made to lie down*) so that You can refresh me...I pray that it will not be a "forced" rest, but rather a *green pastures, still waters* rest. I praise You for Your refreshment. You know this lamb better than I know myself. You know me. How well do I know You?" (Personal journal – January 7, 13, 1989)

Is it just me or does it seem like somebody hit the fast-forward button on the DVD player of life? I remember the winter of 1972 when the Lord allowed me to be flat on my back for 28 days (pneumonia). I prayed almost daily, "Lord, help me to let go and rest quietly at Your feet in complete attention to You." The time spent with the Lord during this "forced" rest was awesome and the lessons learned invaluable. My solitude broke time, broke words, and broke me. And during that time of rest I was healed and mended, physically and spiritually. And I continued in the following years to practice those lessons, right? WRONG!! It wasn't very long at all before I was back at my most consistent exercise program called "The Be-All-Things-To-All-People" fitness regimen. How many times does the "rut" of religious activity numb my soul until I find myself in need of spiritual refreshment—a fresh touch of God Who is continuing to work within me? Often this occurs to me in the waning weeks of winter and I realize that I need to slow down, pull out of that rut and take a different path. And sometimes it means just getting away from it all, literally. It is at those times that I seek out a place where there are no demands upon my time, where I can find spiritual renewal and slow down and be quiet and know that HE is God!!

> "Am I so seldom in one place that my friends regard me as a phantom? Am I so consistently on the move that my family is beginning to question my existence? Do I take pride in my frenzy at the expense of my faith? *Man is a mere phantom as he goes to and fro. He bustles about but only in vain. He heaps up wealth; not knowing who will get it.* (Psalm 39:6)" (Personal journal – May 7, 1993)

Lord, why is it that even though I walk in Your grace, I still carry the load on my own back? I've prayed that prayer many times. I came across another prayer some years ago:

> "Here is a prayer to be said when the world has gotten you down and you feel rotten and you're too doggone tired to pray; and you're in a big hurry, and besides you're mad at everybody—HELP!!"

Interesting prayer, don't you think? It's almost like hearing His voice saying to me, "My, son, slow down; cool it! Admit your need." Good counsel; tough to carry out. Asking for help is smart; so why don't I do that more often? Ah, my number one nemesis answers that question—PRIDE. Pride is nothing more than my stubborn unwillingness to admit need. That inner voice inside of me (no, I'm not talking about the Holy Spirit) keeps saying, "Prove it to them. You can do it; you don't need anybody's help."

And the result is impatience, irritation, anger, resentment, longer periods of time between meaningful minutes in God's Word, longer hours of working, less and less laughter, inflexibility, and precious few moments of prayer or prolonged meditation (if any).

I remember a little conversation I had with myself a few years ago. I said, "Self, there is no way you can keep going at this pace year after year and stay effective for the Kingdom. You are h-u-m-a-n and nothing more. Slow down and give yourself a break. Stop trying to cover all the bases! RELAX!! Since when is a bleeding ulcer or a heart attack a sign of spirituality? Since when is a 70-hour work week a mark of efficiency?" Perhaps I need to use that 4-letter word more often. God loves to hear me use it—HELP!!

Is it time to stop for a moment and acknowledge to God that I can't handle everything? Do I need to be reminded that He already knows what's happening? Do I need to be nudged into believing that He's there (always has been), ready to take my hand and help me through this day and its situations, some that I'd rather not deal with? I love the prayer of Brennan Manning: (Brennan is a former priest in the Catholic Church who battled alcoholism) "May all your expectations be frustrated; may all your plans be thwarted; may all your desires be withered into nothingness that you may experience the powerlessness and poverty of a child and sing and dance in the compassion of God Who IS Father, Son and Spirit. Amen."

The killer of God-led ministry is BUSYNESS. It's insidious pace leaves no room for time alone with the Lord. There is no time for reflection and quietness. Corrie ten Boom said, "Beware the barrenness of a busy life." Times of quiet and solitude are often disdained by men (by me) because it often reveals my inward poverty. I came across something I wrote many years ago, "I don't feel at peace today. I feel restless. The peace that Jesus speaks of seems impossible for me to embrace most of the time, much less at all times and in every way. When I look back on times when I have known the peace of God, they have two things in common—1) My heart has been quiet; 2) There has been some reminder of Your creative power. Lord, please help me find a peace that goes beyond these moments. In the middle of hecticness, please remind my heart that the quiet place where You handle the details does exist. Don't let me fool myself into thinking that I have everything under control. Humble me and remind me that even I can experience Your peace at all times and in every way."

No pastor (no Christian) can depend on anyone else to feed his feelings of fulfillment. It's an inside job, blessed by God. Psalm 43:5—*Why are you so downcast, O my soul? Why so disturbed within me? Put your hope in God, for I will yet praise him, my Savior and my God.* I have the power to slay my own weariness, not by "bucking up", but by looking at life from my Father's viewpoint. I have discovered that I become too busy because I want to be busy. I realize that I can very well cut out a great deal of "busy" activity in my life and not seriously damage my productivity for the Lord.

Finding time for me is a never-ending challenge. The world is constantly encroaching—an important meeting, my grandkid's concert, special services at the church, a new project—the list is endless. Again and again I fall prey to the pressure of busyness, and before I know it I'm almost resenting the very things I once enjoyed. I haven't been practicing the balance I've preached so often about. I've not made time for myself—for solitude. Finally, out of necessity, I shut out the world for a few hours, sometimes even a night, and just rest in Him. And then it comes back to me. And yet even in the midst of this time of calm, I am severely tempted to turn on the radio or pick up my cell phone and call someone. Performing is always easier than resting in the presence of God. When God brings me into a time of waiting and doesn't give me the quick answer right now, I will fill the time with busyness. But God just wants me to WAIT. Solitude wants to be a stranger, and I can hardly bring myself to seek it out. But with determined deliberateness I discipline myself to be still. A half a hundred thoughts wrestle for my attention—phone calls I need to make, things I need to do, chores I should be accomplishing. And as I discipline myself to be still and resist the temptation to tackle life's tasks right now; bit by bit I feel the tensions slip away. The noise of the world is pushed back for a while. Even discordant voices within me grow quiet. And in the silence of God's presence I am renewed. I love the prayer: "Dear God, forgive us our noise. Give us the courage to say 'no' to the noisemakers in the church so we can listen to the Holy Spirit speaking to us…"

"I'm not sure I can handle that early hospital call this morning; but He can.

I don't think I can face that staff meeting today; but He can.

The work to be accomplished before I sleep tonight, I'm just not sure that I can do it; but He can. I cannot handle another wedding rehearsal this month; but He can.

I just can't give myself (piece by piece) to anybody else; my counseling load is just too great for me; but not for Him. Here we go, Lord."

(Personal journal – 1-28-2000)

A couple of years ago I made a list of my 10 favorite sounds; those that impacted my senses in a relaxing and even renewing way. Not only do they provide a challenging exercise for my mind, but they sharpen my appreciation for some golden moments in time.

1.) My backyard early in the morning

2.) My wife (or) daughters (or) grandkids saying, "I love you."

3.) The crackling of a campfire at night

4.) The silence of Christmas Eve after a midnight service

5.) The sound of the woods in the Fall

6.) The surf along the Gulf of Mexico

7.) Inspired rifts filling in from Greg Weiler's guitar

8.) A group of Haitian children singing

9.) Canadian geese flying overhead

10.) A mountain stream moving rapidly over rocks

I cannot help but wonder how many holy moments I've missed simply because I let weariness or busyness keep me from the moment. We are in constant danger of becoming enslaved by the very things that were supposed to make this life more convenient—laptops, fax machines, Blackberry cell phones. They threaten to take us hostage and no matter where I go, my work goes with me. Never say that you have no time. What we lack is NOT time; but rather HEART. Once we begin wisely allotting time for reading and reflection, wondering and writing, we shall soon notice the reward. Life becomes less pressured. Christ, not the clock on the wall, becomes the center of our lives. Amazing, isn't it? We seem to accomplish more because our energy is not siphoned into pockets of useless worry. What a joy it is to make time our servant instead of becoming enslaved to it.

So what have I learned after almost 65 years of life? OK, I confess. I'm still in the process of learning it…sort of.

1. We constantly walk in His grace while carrying our own loads on OUR backs

2. The killer of God-led ministry is busyness

3. I become too busy because I want to be busy

4. Often what we lack is not time; but rather heart

In the name of Jesus Christ, who was never in a hurry, I pray, O Father that You will slow me down, for I know that I live too fast. With all eternity before me, make me take the time to live—time to get acquainted with You, time to enjoy Your blessings and Your creation, and time to know those around me. May I have the time to love wholeheartedly, be surprised, and give thanks and praise; and then I will discover the fullness of my life.

Chapter Seven – Compassion Over Criticism

"Compassionate intercession leaves you neither time nor inclination to pray for your own 'sad, sweet self.'" (Oswald Chambers)

Compassion is God's call to intercession for others. We are never called to fault finding. It is impossible to fervently pray one way and live another. You cannot pray for another person and then turn around and criticize him. If you are still the same miserable, grouchy person set on having your own way and constantly finding the flaws in others, then it is a lie to say that God has saved and sanctified you.

Jesus said, *Judge not, that you be not judged.* (Matthew 7:1) Criticism is a part of the natural man, but in the spiritual domain nothing is accomplished by criticism. Actually, when you stop to think about it, the Holy Spirit is the only One in a position to criticize anyone. When I am in a foul mood; it makes me hard and vindictive and cruel, and leaves me with the flattering notion that I am a superior person. If I am truly open to the leading of the Lord in my life, when I see negative things in others, God will reveal those identical negative things in me. It is virtually impossible to enter into fellowship with God when I am sporting a critical attitude. Only the Spirit has the right to judge my brother. My role is to be Christ's and to become my brother's servant. Why is it that we Christians seem to be so busy demonizing each other that we have forgotten to do what Jesus told us to do—to love each other and bear witness of that love wherever we go? Albert Einstein wrote, "Great spirits have always encountered violent opposition from mediocre minds." What is it that makes the difference in me? How do I become a "great spirit" for the Lord?

My purpose on this planet is TO GLORIFY GOD!! I've preached it for years; it is THE purpose of the existence of the Church. I will never become small-minded about anything when I understand His purpose for me. Since I became His disciple I cannot be as independent as I used to be. The purpose of God is not to answer my prayers (or my whims), but by my prayers I come to discern the mind of God. Know what? God is not all that concerned about my plans. Surprise!! Members of the body of Christ (that's you and me) are to focus on what is best for others around us, rather than the rightness of our personal opinions.

Isn't it interesting how compassion shown toward others in the world goes against our human nature? Showing compassion to my fellow man just isn't a natural thing for me to do. How do we cultivate that compassionate spirit within us as we live each day in a careless, self-absorbed world? I think a lot of it is centered in doing the unexpected. We've heard in recent years about being involved in random acts of kindness. The concept pretty much started in the Vineyard movement; and now even the world has picked up on it. A 5th grade class in LaPorte was directed to a random acts of kindness website in their computer lab. How about that? And being compassionate in our world today is a major risk. It might not be accepted well. We might be criticized or thought to be weird. I think showing compassion is another place where our faith comes in. It involves believing the Lord against all odds and obeying Him even if our "compassion action" backfires. And when we are involved in acts of compassion, there are times it will backfire. The throngs will not always look at us with adoring gratefulness. The spirit of compassion in you and me plays a major role in our day to day relationship to the Lord. I think it's probably easier to die for our faith than to lay down our lives day in and day out.

> "Lord, help me not to be self-absorbed so that I simply can't imagine a world where I am not present. Convict me of the fact that God really doesn't need my help. He was doing just fine before I came along and will be doing fine long after I've passed from this time and space I occupy. You do as You please, Father and you do it without my help, thank you. Lord, help me to continue to rely upon and bask in Your grace. Drive me to apply grace to others. There is always one fact more in every man's life about which I know nothing. I am so quick to criticize smaller things in others and ignore greater matters in myself. I am so quick to feel the weight of suffering that others cause me; but blow off the suffering I cause to others. Let nothing be great to me—nothing high, nothing pleasing, nothing acceptable—except YOU. Lord, thank you for teaching me flexibility in Your grace. I have never met the man that I would give up on after discerning what lies in me apart from Your grace. I am learning that the closer I come to You, I find that my judgment about others is quite different from Your judgment. Help me embrace Your contentment in me. Keep on teaching me to always think well and commendably of others and have no opinion of myself. What is higher or more important or more filled with life and vitality than to love You and love others around me?" (Personal journal – December 16, 2002)

James 4:11 says *Brothers, do not slander one another.* Literally that says that we are not to speak against each other. Perhaps you remember the childhood rhyme that goes, "Sticks and stones may break my bones, but words will never hurt me." Even at a very young age I knew there was something drastically wrong with that statement; because words DO hurt. In fact, sometimes they can hurt much more than physical abuse. Words are powerful! In the third chapter of his letter, James has already told us how evil our tongues can be. And in James 4:11-12 he tells us pretty plainly why we should not speak against one another. As is his usual habit, James uses the command form of the verb. It is, in fact, a "do it now with urgency" command. Simply put, we need to stop criticizing each other! And to quit doing that we have to continually be evaluating our attitudes toward each other. Do we build each other up; or do we tear each other down? When we're ready to criticize another are we remembering God's royal law of love? Remember what James said in 2:8? – *If you keep the royal law found in scripture, "Love your neighbor as yourself," you are doing right.* If we are serious about walking the walk that God intends for us then we need to know and practice one of his very practical principles—DON'T SHOOT YOUR OWN GUYS!

The heart of James' message is "stop it; stop bad-mouthing each other immediately!" It may be OK to pick your friends, but not to pieces. John Wesley was preaching a sermon on the parable of the talents. After the service one lady told him that her talent was speaking her mind; to which Wesley answered, "I'm certain, Sister, that God wouldn't object at all if you buried that talent."

Loving my brother means treating him the way I like to be treated; speaking to him the way I like to be spoken to (Jesus said that). But instead of following what Jesus teaches us we often try to inflate ourselves by cutting one another down. Backbiting is always a subtle form of exalting ourselves. How many times do we gossip and talk behind another's back and criticize them, all in the name of concern, and the church ends up being damaged. God has always been aware of the harsh critical spirit in our world that is dominated by those who find fault with just about everything. A lot of trouble in our world (as well as in the church) is caused by the lethal combination of narrow minds and big mouths. James in 4:11 goes on to say that when I speak against my neighbor I am literally *sitting in judgment of the Law.* How can that be? Again, scripture commands me to *love my neighbor as myself.* When I exhibit my critical spirit, I, in fact, place myself above the Law. I am saying by my actions that the Law is worthless; it's invalid. The Living Bible says *when you criticize you are fighting against God's law of loving one another, declaring it is wrong.* The Peterson paraphrase says *you're supposed to be honoring the Message, not writing graffiti all over it.*

I remember when the new Cleveland Avenue extension opened up not too far from our house. What a great new 5-lane road! But it really ticked me off that the posted speed limit was 30 mph. What was that all about? So what do I do? Hey, it's a wide open space out in the country. It's a brand new road and I have a hard time getting my car to go 30 mph. So I drove 50 mph (or more). The speed limit signs are clearly posted. There is no doubt as to what is expected of me, but I still drive 50 mph. What am I saying about that law? I'm basically saying that it's not valid and I think it's a stupid law and I shouldn't have to obey it! So I don't. I ignore the law. That's exactly the point James is making here. God has clearly stated His law to us—*Love one another.* But we ignore it by cutting each other down, which in essence says to God, "This law is dumb and I'm not going to follow it!" That is sitting in judgment of the law. And in James 4:12 he says *there is only one Lawgiver and Judge, the one who is able to save and destroy. But you—who are you to judge your neighbor?* Translation: There is only ONE JUDGE; and you ain't Him!

Christian author, F.B. Meyer writes, "When we see a brother or sister in sin, there are two things we do not know. First, we don't know how hard he or she tried not to sin. Second, we do not know the power of the forces that assailed him or her." Actually there's a third thing we don't know. We don't know what we would have done in the same circumstances. And do you know WHY we don't know these things? Because we're not God. God sees everything. He looks into our hearts and evaluates our actions and attitudes. It is God who judges and gives life. Who are we to think that we can play God? Who are we to think that we can do better than God? Who are we to pass judgment on anybody? That's like a smoker telling an alcoholic that he has a terrible habit. We are in no position to judge each other.

So how do we respond to truth like that? Maybe each of us needs to look back on this past week and think about the times we've criticized a brother or sister. Maybe it transpired in your home or your workplace or in your church. What have you whispered about someone? What kind of negative or harsh words have you said about another? James says to us—"STOP IT!" Examine yourself. Be vigilant before you speak. Humble yourself. Don't try to elevate yourself by bringing others down. As a matter of fact, James also says in chapter 4, *Humble yourself and let God lift you up.* I think I would rather be busy in Kingdom work so that I wouldn't have the time to be criticizing anyone else.

In the New Testament letter to the Romans, Paul says that before putting on Jesus Christ *your mouths were full of cursing and bitterness like an open garbage heap.* But then Paul says, after you put on Jesus Christ, what a difference. In Romans 10 he says *you confess with your mouth that Jesus Christ is Lord.*

A story is told of John Bunyan, author of *Pilgrim's Progress.* When he was a little boy he used to sit on the porch of his home and listen to his mother and three or four other women sitting there on a beautiful summer afternoon just talking. They talked of the things of God. They shared how they were comforted and refreshed by the love of Jesus Christ and how wonderful it was to be in His service. John Bunyan later recounted how listening to those conversations made an enormous impact upon his life. Isn't that great? But, what if these women had been critically speaking of others? What if Bunyan had grown up in your home, listening to your daily conversations? Would that be just as great?

Lessons learned? – I hope!!

1. You cannot pray for another person and then turn around and criticize him.

2. The negative things I see in others, God will reveal those identical negative things in me.

3. I will never become small-minded about anything when I understand His purpose for me.

4. Good church rule: Don't shoot your own guys!

Chapter Eight – Action Over Academia

In the Spring of 1967 I was preparing to be ordained into the ministry as a pastor. It was an event and passage of my life for which I felt tremendously unprepared and inadequate. Before that service on a Sunday evening, April 23, Lester Martin, an old elder from my week-end student pastorate in Pence, Indiana, pulled me aside and said, "Remember son, when you preach, you will be speaking to ordinary people." Thank you, Lester for that tremendous gem of wisdom for one such as I who was crammed full of theological insight to share with the multitudes. So I stuffed what I considered to be his "alka-seltzer wisdom" in my bag of expendable advice and went forth to be ordained.

As it turned out, in my early years of arrogant ignorance, I really didn't know much about ordinary people. You know, it really was more fun when I knew everything. I was ripe with scholarly insights and tuned into my theology. I was honing my craft of sermonizing, but I was not tuned in to the ordinariness of the people who were listening to my "up-in-the-ivory-tower" preaching. I was raised in a "church culture" where nobody really worried all that much about Jesus as long as He could be kept tucked quietly away safe and sound in our theology books and church traditions. But you know what? There will always be unrest if you try to let Him out! Oswald Chambers wrote, "Spiritual truth is learned by atmosphere (a perception of what we can only do in the Lord), not by intellectual reasoning." Our spiritual capacity is never based upon education or intellect. It is ALWAYS based upon the promises of God! While our knowledge increases, wisdom to know how to use it can come only from God. Proverbs 2:6 says *the Lord gives wisdom; from his mouth comes knowledge and understanding.* True wisdom does not come from books. It comes from THE BOOK!

In Acts 13, Paul and his companions were ministering in Pisidian Antioch. After reading from the Law and the Prophets, the spiritual leaders there had a special request. *Brothers, if you have a message of encouragement for the people, please speak.* (Acts 13:15) Isn't that the need? Isn't that the inner desire of all of us ordinary people? If you have a message of encouragement for me, please share it!

Years ago, a poignant and painful book and film came out entitled *Ordinary People.* It's a story that gives a new definition of human ordinariness. A perfectionist mother tries so hard to crowd her little world into her complete control, and finds that she can't cope when her favorite son dies. He drowns, and her power to love drowns with him. Her other son cannot deal with his guilt for being alive when his brighter, "better" brother was dead. The people closest to him are hanging out there all alone, out of his reach. Ordinary people. To be ordinary is to be too weak to cope with the terrible stuff that is too much for mere humanity. Ordinary people are non-heroes, limited folk who are afflicted with the disease of being overwhelmed with life.

The gospel is not primarily for eager scholars, but for hurting people in need of healing. *If you have a message of encouragement for me, please share it* is the inner request of ALL ordinary people just like you and me. Sometimes we get the idea that all the people in the Bible walked slowly around the highways and byways, in white robes, seeking those out to whom they could do good deeds, continually folding their hands with a glowing halo reflected over them, constantly saying, "Verily, verily; behold I cometh." There were people in the synagogue where Paul preached that day who were hurting deeply inside; no different from the average church service today. Charles Spurgeon said, "There is a hurting soul in each and every pew." There are people in your congregation (maybe sitting right next to you) who have lost loved ones, are having marriage problems or problems with their kids, drinking problems, loss of employment, and the list goes on. There were even people there that day who sometimes got sick and threw up. I wonder how many times the church has given the impression that we perfect saints of God never get dirty or sweaty or sick. The Galatian letter tells us that Paul was sick when he first arrived in this area. So Paul preaches to a bunch of "needing help plain old humans." *If you have a message of encouragement for me, please share it.* Ordinary people. And ordinary people are people who live on the edge, just a step behind the line that separates us from those who fall apart at the seams. For many, survival is often the biggest success story we dare hope for. Ordinary people are the ones who need to be reassured that it might still be OK even when everything seems to be horribly wrong.

I wonder how many times we put unreal expectations upon each other in the body of Christ. If everyone isn't dancing to the spectacular music of the Spirit and performing as great spiritual athletes with shoulders strong to bear the burdens of global injustice and carrying out the heroic mandates of the Word of God, we criticize their lack of spirituality and quality of their faith. We point the finger of knowledgeable superiority and let them know that they're just not "deep enough." And yet our churches are filled with people who are secretly praying, "Oh, God, I don't think I can get through the week; HELP ME*!!*" I remember years ago talking to a woman who visited our church. She said, "All of your people here seem so together. I'm not sure I can relate." The good news is that she's still around today because she got to know us.

When people in the body don't open their hearts to each other, we wither away. Why is it that we hold those things we could share with others so tightly to ourselves? Why do we hide our true persons behind the facades of phoniness? Our pastor, Kevin Galloway, recently wrote in his blog, "The part of us that is compelled to share and the part of us that is compelled to hold on to things too tightly is the DNA of our spiritual make-up. What would it look like if we actually did the things we talk and sing about? What would it look like to have the favor (Acts 2:47) of our culture instead of the hate that seems to come at us because we seem to live so differently than the teachings of the Jesus that draws men to Himself?" *If you have a message of encouragement for me, please share it.*

Kierkegaard wrote, "Many choose to lock the door of their heart because they want to live in the wretched doghouses of their lives." In that same chapter (Acts 13) Paul preaches, *Look, you scoffers, wonder and perish because I am going to do something in your days that you would never believe, even if someone told you.* Scripture tells us that God's calling to all of us ordinary people will be extraordinary. The words of scripture (and of our Lord) are given to us to get all of us religious professionals off the fence of theory and academics and into the world of reality (where true Christianity is put into action). Our Lord is calling us to action! Jack London (I remember reading his *Call of the Wild* when I was a boy) has written: "I would rather be ashes than dust. I would rather that my spark should burn out in a brilliant blaze than it should be stifled by dry-rot. I would rather be a superb meteor, every atom in me in magnificent glow, than a sleepy and permanent planet. The proper function of man is TO LIVE, not to exist. I shall not waste my days trying to prolong them. I shall use my time."

So we all sit here in church. A man and woman, sitting straight-faced, looking good, saying the right things in public, in reality hate each other for letting the romance in their marriage collapse; day by day walking through that tiring treadmill of tidy tedium. A widow, whispering "amens" to every promise of scripture being quoted, frightened to death because the beast of inflation against her fixed income is devouring her savings. A father, the congregational model of parental firmness, fuming in the suspicion of his own fatherly failure because he can't stomach, much less understand the rebellious antics of his slightly wacky son. An attractive young woman absolutely paralyzed because she just found out she has breast cancer. A middle-aged guy, drives a new Mercedes, an obvious "Christian success story", miserably trapped in his job and wondering if he will ever have the guts to tell his boss to take this lousy job and….well, you know. A teenager wondering how to tell her parents that she's pregnant. A submissive wife of a church leader terrified because she knows she has to face up to her closet alcoholism. And there are so many others. *If you have a message of encouragement, please share it.*

Summary:

1. The ministry of the church is to ordinary people

2. Our spiritual capacity is never based upon education or intellect…It is always based upon the promises of God

3. The gospel is not primarily for eager scholars, but for hurting people in need of healing

4. When people in the body don't open their hearts to each other, we wither away

5. *If you have a message of encouragement, please share it.* (Acts 13:15)

Karl Barth made the insightful statement, "All of my theological studies are summed up thusly—'Jesus loves me this I know; for the Bible tells me so.'"

Chapter Nine – St. Valentines Over the County Clerk

"How did I become so fortunate as to marry a woman such as you? Luck? I don't think so. God's hand? I have absolutely no doubt. I thank the Lord every day of my life for His bringing us together."

(Personal Journal – Our Wedding Anniversary – August 12, 1980)

An ancient Greek legend tells of a Cyprian king named Pygmalion who found a unique way of solving potential marital differences. He became so frustrated with his inability to find the right woman to marry that he decided to sculpt one. Out of the most exquisite ivory he could find, he fashioned the woman of his dreams. When he was done, he bowed and prayed and the ivory woman miraculously came to life. Pygmalion took her as his wife and they lived happily ever after.

It's easy to see why that legend endured. Who wouldn't like to custom-design their mate? Wouldn't it be fun to take the chisel and chip away until you had the man or woman of your dreams? And interestingly enough that's what many of us try to do to our spouses. We chip away at what we perceive to be each other's rough edges; those flaws that make her think or behave or respond differently from me. I mean, if I can just get her to be more like me, I know we can have a decent marriage.

There is an interesting custom in our weddings today. It is included in about 90% of the ceremonies I conduct. It's called the unity candle. It is symbolic of the couple becoming one flesh. Often the mothers of the respective bride and groom light the end candles. Then at a certain point in the wedding, the bride and groom will each take their candle and together light the center candle. What happens next always amuses me. After the center candle is lit, the bride and groom many times blow out the smaller candles they are holding.

Now I'm not sure I would have married my wife of almost 43 years if I had known that even before the echoes of our vows had faded away she had planned to snuff me out! I certainly understand the concept of oneness. But the deeper, scriptural meaning of marriage is that two people become one so that they may each become more than they could ever have become by themselves. Spiritual oneness is the goal. But our two-ness doesn't cease to exist. Our separate personalities don't die. I think we sometimes give couples a false picture in marriage. We say, "You are to become one." And when that doesn't magically happen (and it won't just magically happen), our mentality today says, "Well, we must not be compatible; so we'll just split."

Allow me to let you in on a little secret. The two of you aren't compatible. Marriage is the art and developed skill of two incompatible people learning and growing to BECOME compatible. Make no mistake about it, all of us fallen "plain old humans" living on this fallen planet are incompatible!

A man came into my office years ago. He said, "I'm going to get a divorce. I just don't love my wife anymore and you can't stay married to someone you don't love." And I replied, "Why not?" (That always gets their attention). Don't tell me that you have always loved your wife/husband. And I'm talking about biblically defined love now. Helen and I were watching the news one evening (we had been married a few years). There was a report of a guy being beat up by his wife with a baseball bat. I said, "Can you imagine a woman doing that to her husband?" And Helen said, "Oh yeah!"

It's interesting how Christians reject the "big bang" theory in creation, but we readily embrace it in the area of what we call "true love." Love is a commitment to remain loyal and faithful even when we don't feel like it. Marriage is a relationship instituted by God and based upon HIS standards. Do we get it? In marriage, God's Word is the standard!! And our churches need to be at the forefront of telling it like it is.

"I cherish the treasure, the treasure of you;

Lifelong companion, I give myself to you.

God has enabled me to walk with you faithfully,

And cherish the treasure, the treasure of you."

(John Mohr)

> "I praise God for bringing this song into our lives at this time in our marriage. What a truth it proclaims concerning the way I feel about you, my darling. I give all praise and glory to God for you! What a fantastic 22 years I've had with my treasure, the treasure of you. Happy Anniversary, Honey."

(Personal Journal – August 12, 1988)

Ephesians 5:21 says *Submit to one another out of reverence for Christ.* Literally, honor Jesus by submitting to each other in the marriage. And then there is that next verse that women love, *Wives, submit to your husbands as to the Lord.* Some can get so bent out of shape when they read that. And the basic reason is that too many of us are spending too much time focusing on our personal rights, rather than understanding what lordship is all about.

Sociologist, Carle Zimmerman in his book, *Family and Civilization,* recorded his keen observations as he compared the disintegration of various cultures with the parallel decline of family life in those cultures. Eight specific patterns of domestic behavior typified the downward spiral of each culture Zimmerman studied.

1. Marriage loses its sacredness and is frequently broken by divorce

2. Traditional meaning of the marriage ceremony is lost

3. Feminist movements greatly increase

4. Increase of public disrespect for parents and authority in general

5. An acceleration of juvenile crime, promiscuity and general rebellion

6. Refusal of people within traditional marriages to accept family responsibilities

7. A growing desire and acceptance of adultery; it is no longer disgraceful

8. Increasing interest in and spread of sexual perversion and sex-related crime

May I say with all of the fervency that I can muster that we men must share a great portion of the blame here? When Ephesians 5:23 says *for the husband is the head of the wife as Christ is the head of the church, his body, of which he is the Savior,* I am blown away. It's interesting to me that some women get uptight with that scripture, and yet the real "heavy" of the emphasis here is upon men getting their act together. How can my wife get under my spiritual leadership and my protection (which is what "submission" is all about) if I don't provide that leadership and protection? Remember, this is a lordship issue! And the balance of it all is Ephesians 5:28—*Husbands ought to love their wives as their own bodies. He who loves his wife loves himself.* This chapter of scripture lays out for us the beautiful principle of mutual submission in marriage. When a Christian man submits himself to Christ and lets Him be Lord of his life, he WILL love his wife. And when a Christian woman submits herself to Christ and lets Him be the Lord of her life she WILL submit herself to her husband. When there are marriage problems among Christians, it is a LORDSHIP problem!

I like what one author has written, "If you want to succeed in marriage, learn to adjust and bend toward your partner. Keep your expectations of each other realistic. Keep your expectations of the Lord idealistic. And remember that a happy marriage is the union of two good forgivers." I wrote that down many, many years ago and it has kept my "head in the game" often.

"Unless we are particularly heroic or saintly persons (which I am not), each of us needs a relationship with another person who loves and seeks and trusts in a simple way. Such a relationship becomes enormously supportive to us. The rigorous demands of such a coupling are great. They include the gift of oneself, one's time, one's preferences, the nakedness and honesty which are more than and beyond the price many are willing to pay. But the longer I live with you, my darling, the more and more I am willing to pay that price. Anyone who has been so graced (as I have) with a true love relationship knows the cost and knows the worth. And he knows the ridiculousness of complaining about the cost of such a relationship, when deep down he understands that possession ("the treasure of you") is a priceless one. There is no way to measure its worth.

Anticipating the beginning of our 28th year together."
(Personal journal – August 12, 1993)

In looking at the Lord's standard of marriage, I believe that there are three key concepts to consider.

ONE – The Lord's standard is COMMITMENT.

Our culture has big problems with what I like to call the dreaded "C" word. Marriage is a promise that I'm going to stay with this person I've committed my life to. I'm going to take responsibility to make it happen. One of America's leading psychotherapists writes, "The reason marriages are falling apart today is because people are basically lazy." It's true. I've never told a couple in marriage counseling anything they didn't already know. The problem is that we are (as James has taught us in the New Testament) *hearers of the word and not DOERS of the word.* You show me a Christian couple who is having problems and I'll show you a couple who has the resources to solve those problems. It's just that so many are too lazy to DO the things they have to do to make it work.

When scripture tells husbands and wives to love each other the text is literally telling you to DO the things that lovers do. *Agape* love in the Bible is an action word. It's not a feeling. It's something to be done. If every married couple would daily DO loving things for each other, I guarantee that they will experience the feelings that are often identified as being in love. If you are experiencing marriage problems right now, if you would DO 10 things every day that you would do if you "really were in love", I guarantee that within a month or so you WILL be in love with your mate. If all of you precious couples start obeying the Lord and start doing the things for each other that lovers do it won't be long before you start feeling those things that lovers feel. When you invest in a relationship, your heart will follow. That's exactly the same principle Jesus was referring to when He said *where your treasure is, there will your heart be also.*

The key is not "R" for romance; it is "C" for commitment. I was romantically turned on by Helen when we got married. I was NOT in love with her as I biblically understand love today. There had better be more than just romantic attraction involved here. I'm not against romance. My wife will tell you that I'm very romantic. But the average individual falls romantically in love six times before marriage. By the way, the same potential is there after marriage. (Red flag caution)

Agape love is something that matures between two people who are committed to the same things in life. When you get married you need to be asking, "What's the most important thing in your life?" That's why scripture tells us not to be unequally yoked together. If you are a Christian, then the most important thing in your life is Jesus. So how can you become one flesh with someone who does NOT see Jesus as the most important thing in life? There's another principle involved here—"Two people intensely committed to the same thing will develop an intense commitment to each other." That's why I will have the "hots" for Helen after 42 years. I love her more today, she is better looking to me today than the day I married her. And if you guys don't feel that way about your wives you had better take a good look at yourself. I have a strong sense that there needs to be a lot of repentance in the church today. Helen and I love each other more because we both love Jesus more.

TWO – The Lord's standard is FAITHFULNESS.

It has been said, "Faithfulness is an inner conviction of being overwhelmed by God." If God is overwhelming you, you WILL be faithful in your marriage. I've had guys sit in my office and tell me that God is leading them to leave their wife.

And I have no qualms whatsoever telling them that that is a lie from the pit of Hell.

It seems almost silly to say this, but in our culture today, probably not. Every Christian married couple needs to make a mutual commitment to make sure that your sexual relationship is everything God meant it to be. And that means that you commit yourselves to sexual faithfulness (period). If my wife is going to be swept off of her feet by a knight in shining armor then I'm going to have to do the sweeping. If I'm going to have my romantic intimacy dreams come true my wife is the one who is to make it happen. Helen and I believe that we owe it to each other to do everything we can to fulfill our intimacy needs, and no one else is ever involved in that. When another party becomes involved in the meeting of those needs, that kind of unfaithfulness rips apart and tears at the cleaving and bonding that God has created and blessed. Paul writes *since there is so much immorality in the culture, each man should have his own wife, and each woman her own husband. The husband should fulfill the intimacy needs of his wife, and likewise the wife should fulfill the intimacy needs of her husband. The wife's body does not belong to her alone but also to her husband. In the same way, the husband's body does not belong to him alone, but also to his wife. Do not deprive each other except by mutual consent and for a brief time only so that you may devote yourselves to prayer* (I guess that rules out using sex to manipulate my mate). *Then come together again so that Satan will not tempt you because of your lack of self control.* (1 Corinthians 7:2-6)

"'Romance!' There are those who will say, 'Romance is only for the young.' OK, I'll go along with that to a point, which is if all we mean by romance is moonlight and music. But if we're talking about a relationship in which two individuals are committed to one another for life, then that's another matter altogether. And if that relationship is to become all that God wants it to be, then we will live and demonstrate mutual respect, share deep feelings, cultivate kindness, express affection, and cherish one another. That's romance. Isn't it sad that only about 10% of all marriages ever reach their relationship potential (according to statistics, anyway) and the rest struggle along in mediocrity or end in divorce. So many times we can be together, yet very much alone. God intends for marriage to be a special relationship, one in which two people truly become one with each other. It should be where they experience the deepest intimacy, and discover the most complete fulfillment of which they are capable. My precious wife has shown me love time and time again by treating me with respect, by being sensitive to my personal needs (she always senses when I'm hurting), and caring over the years for our children and our home. In marriage, little things can count for so much. Matter of fact, they can make the difference between a mediocre marriage and a really good one; one in which romance is alive and well.

It is not the expensive gifts or the vacations to exotic lands that determine the quality of marital relationship. It is the little things: a card or note found on my desk for no special occasion, stopping by my office when you sense I'm blue; a kind word, a listening ear, the feeling that you really care, and so much more. That's the stuff of which real marriages are made. Thank you for being a REAL wife who has been the key in building a real marriage. Thanks for the little things. *May your fountain be blessed, and may you* (Rick Jones) *rejoice in the wife of your youth. A loving doe, a graceful deer—may her breasts satisfy you always, may you ever be captivated by her love.* (I am). (Proverbs 5:18-19)"

(Personal journal – August 12, 1999)

Just because we got a marriage license from the LaPorte County courthouse, does not guarantee the success of our marriage. Once again, it's a lordship issue! It's about commitment; it's about faithfulness; and it's about…

THREE – The Lord's standard is MUTUAL SERVANTHOOD.

It's called a servant's heart. One southern philosopher said, "When you're complainin' you ain't got no time for confessin'." A good friend of mine told me, "I am convinced that many Christians have fallen into the syndrome of talking about their problems without any intention of finding or applying solutions." The same principles apply in a marriage. We have many complainers, but too few are willing to be servants. At the risk of appearing redundant, may I repeat what I've already stated? When there are marriage problems among Christians, it is a lordship problem. Ephesians 5:25 says that a husband is to love his wife as Christ loved the church. How did Christ love the church? Philippians 2 – *He was willing to give up His majesty and glory and power…He emptied Himself…He loved us so much that He became a SERVANT for us.* That's what Jesus did for me. So if a husband loves his wife in the same way that Christ loved the church, he WILL become a total servant to his wife. And what woman will have any trouble submitting herself to a man who is willingly her servant. It kind of sounds like they are mutually submitted to each other, right?

Ideally, marriage should unite people who are prepared to sacrifice for each other. The wife should be saying, "I am going to sacrifice my life for your well-being. I am going to do everything I can to help you become all that God wills you to be. I am ready to sacrifice my own aspirations and dreams for your sake." And in this ideal marriage the husband will say in response, "Oh no. I am going to sacrifice my life for your well-being. I am going to do everything I can to help you become all that God wills you to be. I am ready to sacrifice my own aspirations and dreams for your sake." Broken marriages begin to mend and communication is reestablished when either one (hopefully both) of the partners is willing to make a breakthrough and say, "Lord, begin with me. I am the one who needs to change and to love more deeply and wisely."

You may believe that your spouse is 100% wrong. But when you stand in the presence of Jesus you will begin to see that you too, have shortcomings. And you will discern where you have failed to accept responsibility for the marital relationship, and you will be able to say, "God, change me." The Christian husband and wife are committed to follow Christ who went all of the way in love, all of the time. So for a start, stop demanding that your partner change his/her ways…Start praying, "Lord, begin the change in me."

The Lord's Standard:

    1.) Commitment

    2.) Faithfulness

    3.) Mutual Servanthood

"A Prayer (from an ancient Jewish prayer)

Blessed are You, O God of our ancestors.

And blessed is Your name in all generations forever.

Let the heavens and the whole creation bless You forever.

You made Adam, and for him you made his wife, Eve as a helper and support.

From the two of them the human race has sprung.

You said, 'It is not good that man should be alone; let us make a helper

        for him like himself.'

Lord, I now take this woman – You have led us together. I take her, not in lust, but in sincerity.

Grant that she and I may find mercy, and that we might grow old together.

And they both said, 'Amen, Amen!'"

(Personal journal – August 12, 2007)

Chapter Ten – Being a Father Over Fathering

If raising kids were easy, it wouldn't have started with something called labor. In ancient China, the people desired security from the barbaric hoards to the north, so they built the Great Wall of China. It was so high they knew no one could climb over it. It was so thick that no one could break it down. So they settled back to enjoy their security. During the first hundred years of the wall's existence, China was invaded three times. Not once did the barbarians break down the wall or climb over it. Each time, at each successful invasion, they marched right through the gate. They were able to do so because they had bribed the gatekeeper. The Chinese were so busy building material security that they neglected to teach integrity to their children who grew up to guard the gates. This account reminds me of Proverbs 19:1—*Better is a poor man that walks in integrity, than he who is perverse in his ways and is a fool.*

My family is where I want to succeed the most. In fact, if I fail here, my life will have been a failure in spite of everything else I may accomplish. And if I succeed here, it will somehow make up for all the failures in my life. My most fervent prayer through the years has been that I would be a godly man and a godly father and godly grandfather. I have never prayed to be a successful pastor or have a successful church. But I have prayed often to be a successful husband and father. I do not present myself as any kind of role-model or perfect dad who has all the answers, because I'm not and I don't!

Briefly consider a scripture with me. Ephesians 6:4—*Fathers, do not exasperate your children; instead bring them up in the training and instruction of the Lord.* Literally that says, "Don't rouse or goad your children to resentment." Don't cause them to become agitated or irritated in spirit because you have overcorrected or over-disciplined them. Don't smother them. But rather nurture and raise them (in other words, DISCIPLE THEM) in the instruction and discipline of the Lord. Do you possess your children or do you nurture them? We have a God-given responsibility here.

Any guy can father a kid. Big deal! But it takes a real man to raise kids God's way. And it's no surprise that we as a nation have NOT been raising our kids God's way. When a man decides to veer off course (yes guys, we choose to thumb our nose at God's standards) everyone in the family pays. America is paying the price today. Men are not following Jesus and there is Hell to pay. I'm really not all that interested in my opinions or your opinions here. I could care less what your way or my way happens to be. Our standard must continue to be GOD'S WAY!! There are two key concepts I want to briefly develop with you. Two little concepts; two time-consuming concepts that will beautifully sum up this whole idea of discipling our kids.

FIRST – Building Wisdom in Our Children

What IS wisdom? Proverbs 1:8—*The fear of the LORD is the beginning of knowledge, but fools despise wisdom and discipline.* Let me sum up the content of scripture regarding this whole parenting thing. The most important ministry we have is to spend the rest of our lives teaching our children to know and love Jesus. And you may say, "Wait a minute. It sounds like we're ramming a lot of religion down our kid's throats here. I'm not sure we ought to be influencing our children in making choices and decisions about religion." Yes, I've actually had people say that to me. And my response is, "Are you kidding?!" The advertising industry will influence them. The media will influence them. The schools will influence them. Friends will influence them. The forces of evil will influence them. We use our efforts to influence the outcomes of our gardens, our pets, our hobbies, sports, and civic clubs. How about our kids? There is a lot of "religion" being taught our there by a culture that is basically become anti-Christian; don't kid yourself.

The National Education Association recently put out a statement: "The solution to the social ills of our society is simply that we need to have our children better educated. We need to give them greater degrees of knowledge." And that is 100% wrong. Something that our world doesn't seem to comprehend is that knowledge apart from wisdom can become a time bomb that will blow up in our faces. I'm not against knowledge. But we live in a techno-society today where there has never been more access to knowledge; more knowledge than you could ever process in a lifetime. What we are lacking in the training of our youth is giving them the wisdom to handle knowledge in a way that will honor God. And I'm talking about training our kids in the wisdom that is to be found in God's Word.

Everything God desires for your child to know—the sovereignty of God, human relationships, money management, work ethics, moral character, integrity, self-control, and peace of mind can be found in God's Word. It would be better for your child to have never read or understood any other book if that came at the cost of not knowing God's Book.

Our nation isn't in the mess it's in today because we don't have enough smart people. Did you know that if you study Proverbs in depth with your family, that by the time your youngster has learned it, he will have completed the most advanced course in human psychology ever written? One psychologist has written—"All the basic characteristics of men and their follies are found in the Book of Proverbs. Not only are the basic characteristics to be found there, but the ends of all of our pursuits as well."

For example, in mastering Proverbs, your child would see a drunk in the gutter and know exactly how that man worked up to that point in life and how to avoid that trap. I'm talking about teachings that clearly lay out the benefit of good conduct as well as the consequences of bad conduct; in other words, teaching that shows us how to behave. One modern author has written—"Ours may be the first generation in civilized times that has NOT raised its young on the principles that are to be found in Proverbs."

There is such a great potential in our children that exists for both great good and great evil. And that's why it is vital for our kids to know the Word of God. God's Word lays the foundation for our passions in life. It reveals the motivation of who we are and what we do. A policeman was watching an elderly lady (she kind of looked like a bag lady) walking about a sidewalk area and picking up something and placing what she found in her bag. He finally confronted her. "Lady, what do you think you're doing?" And she looked up at him and responded, "I'm just picking up the broken glass. I just thought I'd like to take it out of the way of the children's feet." Moms and dads, how we need more and more parents who care about what hurts the children's feet; parents who will guide those feet in paths of wisdom. Psalm 119:105—*Your word is a lamp to my feet and a light for my path.*

SECOND key concept – Building Character in Our Children

A good friend of mine said that the problem with much of the evangelical church today is that we got a whole bunch of selfish adults who are raising a whole bunch of selfish kids. Carl

Sandburg quoted Robert E. Lee giving counsel to parents—
"Please, please, teach your children to deny themselves."

Would you consider with me a brief teaching from Jesus? In
Matthew 19 it tells us that *little children were brought to Jesus
for him to place his hands on them and pray for them. But the
disciples rebuked those who brought them.* (V 13) The custom of
that day was for parents to bring their little ones to the rabbi
for a special blessing. That blessing centered on what that child
would grow up and become IF the parents did their job and
trained them up according to the ways of the Lord. But the
disciples were basically saying, "You know, Jesus really doesn't
have the time for this." Listen to Jesus' response. *"Let the little
children come to me, and do not hinder them, for the kingdom
of heaven belongs to such as these." When he placed his hands on
them* (in other words, when He finished the blessing) *he went
on from there.* (Vv 14-15) Jesus had time for kids. He took the
time. And we had better make the time. As servants of Christ
and as parents under the lordship of Jesus Christ, we had better
have the time! I personally think it's interesting that Matthew
places this beautiful little account directly after Jesus' teaching
on divorce. I don't believe that to be an accident. Children are
always a primary consideration in the building of the lordship
of Jesus Christ into a home. I love this little piece I clipped
from a magazine a few years ago:

> "Take me fishing because my wedding will be sooner than
> you think.
>
> Take me fishing and show me that worms aren't icky.
>
> Take me fishing; you can think about work later.
>
> Take me fishing because I get the giggles when the boat
> bounces.
>
> Take me fishing because my wedding will be sooner than
> you think."

In 1 Thessalonians 2 Paul writes—*For you know that we dealt with each of you as a father deals with his own children; encouraging, comforting, and urging you to live lives worthy of God, who calls you into his kingdom and glory.* (Vv 11-12) The Christians of Thessalonica evidently knew what a father should be. What if you were writing to a group in the inner city of Chicago and said, "Treat each other like fathers in the inner city treat their children"? You may have everyone in the church beat to death, because some fathers do that. Oh wait, that IS how some churches act, isn't it?

Paul tells us:
- A father encourages his children
    > Gives them guidelines to follow; how to pattern their lives
- A father comforts his children
    > Especially when they try to follow those guidelines and fail
- A father urges his children
    > Involves cheering them on; nudging them along; maybe giving them a little pat on the backside; giving them that additional spark they need along the way

I presented this material some time ago and someone said to me, "Man, it sounds like you're talking about discipleship." BINGO!! To disciple someone means that you instruct and train and nurture them toward maturity in Christ. And the most important ministry you will ever have is discipling that youngster of yours, Mom and Dad.

God's way is not man's way. The world's way is to teach your child to get even; God's way is to repay evil with good. The world teaches that you go to college and choose a career that will provide you with financial wealth and then you'll be happy; God's way says, *what shall it profit a man to gain the whole world and lose his own soul.* The world's way is to hoard your wealth for your own future; God's way teaches to invest your wealth in the Kingdom of God's future and trust HIM to take care of yours. Our way, many times, is to try to rely upon routine structured family devotions (I'm not opposed to family devotions); God wants us to be continually training up our children through life experiences and role-modeling. Men desire us to be "event-oriented"; God desires us to be "life-oriented."

What do you teach your kids in the midst of a culture riddled with a shortage of integrity? What are you teaching, not just with your words, but with your daily lifestyle? What do you teach when you cheat on your income tax or gossip about your boss or neighbor or someone at your church? How about when you tell your spouse or child to tell someone on the phone that you're not at home; or you exceed the speed limit and make a joke about it in front of the kids? What do you model when you smile or laugh at questionable humor on the tube? Our children are being "taught" by us at all times. And only sometimes do we use words. Too many are tying the dog up at night and letting the kids run loose.

A few years ago I was babysitting my grandson. He spent quite a bit of time in child care at the local athletic club where his mom worked. He had brought home a toy that belonged to the club. We discussed this fact. He said, "I really like this toy, grandpa, but my heart tells me I have to take it back." Where did he learn that? It didn't come "naturally." Osmosis from some "force" out there didn't just creep into his being. Somebody's teaching something here. We are to be committed to leading our children to the place where they really don't care about what society thinks or what the culture is doing. We are to be committed to placing in their young lives and minds the ability and passion to stand alone and to passionately say, "I want what God wants in my life!"

Scripture talks about "nurturing" our kids. Nurturers need all the help they can get. In the church we are to be involved in encouraging and assisting each other in this task of nurturing our kids. Occasionally I'll talk about MY kids at the church (whether in the Sunday morning children's ministry or my small group of 7th grade boys). And someone will say, "They're not your kids." Yes they are. And my kids and grandkids are yours in the body of Christ. My kids…your kids…my family… your family…OUR family…OUR church/community…WE ARE FAMILY!! That's why Helen and I firmly believe in the ancient Christian tradition of God-parenting.

It's sad, I believe, that this ancient tradition has been abandoned in most, if not all evangelical Christianity. Originally the need for Godparents (or sponsors as they anciently used to be called) arose when people converted to Christ from one of the many pagan religions of the day. There was concern regarding the genuineness of the decision and so converts would be asked to find a Christian friend who would vouch for them. The sponsor would undertake the responsibility of supporting the new convert and ensure that he/she would be helped to become a faithful member of the body of Christ. In the second century the practice evolved into an individual (or married couple) who would support and encourage parents in the raising of their children and helping these youngsters to grow in their faith. Helen and I have been asked to be Godparents for two young people. What a joy. It's an honor, privilege and responsibility to be asked and to assume that role. One tradition asked the prospective Godparents, "This child will depend upon his/her parents and you for the help and encouragement he/she needs. Are you willing to give it to him/her by your prayers, by your example, and by your teaching?" In some circles Godparenting has become little more than gift-giving. That, of course, happens in regular parenting as well. I have learned that the best gift I can give to my Godchildren is time.

Spending time with your Godchildren can and will be a lot more rewarding than simply sending presents. I'm learning more about the process the longer I am involved in it. I continue to pray daily and passionately for both of our Godchildren (one girl and one boy) and am excited about the growing relationship with our newest, our Godson. What a great idea. What a great early church tradition. What a shame it has been largely lost to us. WE ARE FAMILY.

John Wesley said, "Give me 100 men who are sold out to Jesus Christ and I'll change the world." I'd like to change that quote just a bit—"You give me 100 kids who are sold out to Jesus Christ and I'll guarantee we will turn this whole area upside down for Jesus Christ." Anyone can father a kid. I keep praying for a host of men who will become passionate dads for Jesus Christ!!

Chapter Eleven – Faithfulness Over Efficiency

A real turning point for me in my ministry (one of many turning points) was the beginning of 2005 as I was reading Keith Green's biography, <u>No Compromise</u>. It was this particular "turning point" that began to prepare me for transition in my life from serving as senior pastor of a large church to passionately working with children. The heart of Green's message throughout his brief life was 5-fold:

1. Get right with God
2. Witness boldly for Christ
3. Be in the world, not of it
4. Remember the poor
5. Pursue holiness

On January 1 of that year I entered the words in my journal, "May these 5 principles be the driving heart of my ministry in 2005 and beyond." During that year it all came together for me in one principle, one concept, one simple force—FAITHFULNESS!!

True saints persevere! The focus of my life can make the difference between failure and faithfulness. I began to make the above five tenants the focus of everything I did. A.W. Tozer once said, "It is not what a man does that determines whether his work is sacred or secular. It is WHY he does it" (More on this whole "sacred/secular" thing in the next chapter). God began to convict me of the "why" I was doing anything. The foundation of it all was GOD'S FAITHFULNESS! There is absolutely nothing I can do to detract from the faithfulness of God.

"Lord, sometimes I wonder about stuff—my ministry, my family, my priorities, my life. If I allow myself, I could easily be overwhelmed by everything. I often question my competency to pastor a staff and a flock as large as this one. I often second-guess the support I think I have from our leaders, staff, and congregation at large. And lately I even wonder if I'm a good husband and father. Maybe I'm not as good as I thought I was. I wake up 6-7 times a night with a restless spirit. I'm having 2-3 migraines a week now. I have more questions than answers about my ministry; my daughter's marriage is falling apart—yeah, I'm really in control. I guess I need to listen to what I said at the Harvest Praise Festival yesterday. I get to the point where I say, "I can't do it." And you say, "Right, you're exactly where I want you to be." The Lord says to me, "Instead of telling Me what you want to do in your life and how you want Me to do it, will you finally let Me make a way for you? You don't need to know where your life is going when you know that I am leading." (Personal journal – November 19, 2001)

THE VICTORIOUS CHRISTIAN LIFE!! What the heck is that? Most testimonies I've heard through the years about the victorious Christian life do not match my own. You know what I mean, grandiose testimonies; bloated rhetoric. "Once Jesus became my Savior my Christian walk became a picnic in a beautiful garden. My marriage automatically turned into bliss, my physical health flourished, acne disappears and my sinking career suddenly soared." The victorious life is proclaimed to mean that everybody is a winner. Miracles occur, conversions abound and church attendance skyrockets. Shy people become obnoxious and ruptured relationships get healed. And the Cubs win the World Series. (Being a Cub fan since age 4, I always hold on to that one.)

The New Testament depicts another picture of the victorious life; it is Jesus on the cross at Calvary. In some ways the victorious life pictured in scripture reads more like what Brennan Manning calls the "victorious limp." Jesus was victorious not because He never flinched or talked back or questioned, but because He remained FAITHFUL.

Picture yourself as a slave in ancient Rome. You have been brought into the slave market and are now being placed on the auction block. The bidding begins; kind of like a human trafficking ebay. There's a man in the crowd and he joins in the bidding. It's apparent that he badly wants to purchase you. Finally he bids the highest price, wins you, and pays for you. He takes you outside the slave market, and to your utter astonishment, instead of taking you into slavery in his house, he says to you, "You are free. I have paid the price for you. You are a free person." When this happened to you in ancient Rome it meant you were now free to act as your own legal person. You had freedom from seizure of property, free to earn your own living, free to dwell where you wished; complete freedom.

Guess what? Galatians 5:1 says *It is for freedom that Christ has set us free. Stand firm, then, and do not let yourselves be burdened again by a yoke of slavery.* Christ has set you free; SO BE FREE!! We are now free to live as we were created to live. What were we created to do? – GLORIFY GOD!! Now, as believers in Christ and possessors of the Holy Spirit, we can glorify Him.

Galatians 5:6 says *The only thing that counts is faith expressing itself through love.* The battle of the Christian life has always been, not just to believe, but to keep on believing. We grow strong in faith, and we see the actual fulfillment of God's promises in our lives because of this unique place God has given to faith. His grace flows through the channels of His promises, not His commands. His commands do not impart to us the strength to obey, but the Spirit working through His promises do. Without feeding upon the promises of His word, no faith will be strong. Faith is not about the present or about things we can capture right now with a camera. It's about things we can't see; things promised to us by God. Faith produces a conviction that those things are going to happen, even though the scientific method and our senses cannot validate that certainty at the moment. What will happen to our worship leaders, and in turn our church if we come to every corporate worship service with greater faith—a spirit of anticipation and a belief that God is about to do something wonderful? Satan desires us to focus on the problem, not the Provider. Faith is essentially nurtured in us when we just wait in God's presence, and take the time to love Him and listen to His voice. What difficulty or apprehensions are you facing right now at this moment? I wonder what God is waiting to accomplish in your life, in your worship, in your service to Him today, despite those difficulties?

Probably the hardest lesson for me (us) to learn is that our Lord calls us to be unobtrusive disciples, not heroes. The tiniest thing done out of love to Him is more precious to Him than any eloquent preaching of a sermon or excellent playing of an instrument or angelic singing of a song. Why is it that we seem to have this lurking desire within to be exhibitionists for God? Jesus does not want us to be public specimens. He wants us to be so taken up in Him that we never think about ourselves. God calls us not "to walk on water," but to count on the grace of God to live 24 hours a day as a child of God. He calls us to go through our daily routine—even drudgery sometimes—to go through the ordinary, unobtrusive, ignored existence, unnoticed and unnoticeable.

We are called to be exceptional in ordinary things and to be holy in the midst of the unholy! What am I rambling on about here? FAITHFULNESS. What will make authentic disciples of Jesus are not visions or ecstasies or biblical master of chapter and verse or spectacular success in the ministry or an impeccable permanent record in the archives of the denominational headquarters. It is rather a Spirit-produced capacity in me for FAITHFULNESS!! Galatians 5:22 says that the fruit of the Spirit is *FAITHFULNESS!*

Those Christians I have met along the way that have encouraged me the most are those who have failed and learned to live gracefully with their failure as they continue on in their walk. Faithfulness requires the courage to risk everything on Jesus, the willingness to keep growing, and the readiness to risk failure throughout our lives. Winston Churchill said, "Success is never final; failure is never fatal; it is faithfulness that counts." I may be an unspiritual man, but I am determined by the power of the Holy Spirit to be a FAITHFUL unspiritual man. I find more encouragement from my brothers who are pouring themselves into God and risking failure; for I believe they have a better handle on faithfulness than the timid guy who has his ducks all in a row and hides behind the letter of the law never finding what real maturity in Christ is all about. God has not called me to be successful. He has called me to be faithful. And just like all the rest of the fruit (Galatians 5:22-23), I cannot pull this off in the flesh. His Spirit must produce and mature that faithfulness in me. And, I must allow Him to do it!

There's a concept of consistency that is talked about again and again in scripture. And one of the most magnetic, attractive characteristics of Jesus is His consistency.

- When you need Him, He's there
- He's even there when you think you don't need Him
- He's never too early or too late

- He's never in a lousy mood nor will He ask you to call back during office hours
- He's available. With Him there's no old year or new year. He's the same regardless.

Galatians 6:9-10 uses Him as a role-model when it comes to OUR consistency. *Let us not become weary in doing good, for at the proper time we will reap a harvest if we do not give up. Therefore, as we have opportunity, let us do good to all people, especially to those who belong to the family of believers.* Before Helen and I were married, I had a very memorable confrontation with an older brother in the Lord. He totally blew me away with one simple question—"Why do you want to be a preacher of the gospel?" My pat answer was "To win souls and save the lost." His comeback: "Suppose you preach for 30-40 years and nobody believes or responds to your teaching; nobody is ever saved? Will you be a failure?" And I remember trying to barter with God about making me a successful preacher. I prayed for hundreds to come to Jesus because of my preaching. He never promised that. It's a funny thing. The Lord has always given me the understanding that I serve Him regardless of whether anyone responds or not, because He told me to remain faithful. Then this older brother said, "Suppose you preach and preach and no one ever changes their lives; they just keep on living the same old lives; will you be a failure?" And I said nothing. And then he asked, "So you finish your seminary training and you get all prepared to preach and you learn Greek and Hebrew and homiletics and apologetics and hermeneutics and everything else they tell you that you need to know. And after preaching for one week you have a heart attack and die. Will you be a failure?" And I slowly began to realize where he was going. My becoming a preacher of the gospel should not primarily be for the winning of souls or for the accomplishment of any kind of record; not for any kind of "success" in my column at all. My preaching and teaching and ministry are for one reason. My ministry and my walk and my life and my maturing are for one reason only—FOR THE GLORY OF GOD*!!*

I need to embrace this truth so I won't become cynical. I mean, look around you. Aren't there more mouths to feed than bread to go around? Aren't there more wounds to heal than there are physicians? Aren't there more who need truth than those who will tell it? So what do I do? Throw up my hands and walk away? Tell the world around me that I can't help them? NO!! I do not give up. I look up!! I trust; I believe. My optimism isn't hollow. Christ has proven Himself to be worthy. He has shown me that He never fails. That's what makes God, God.

And someday, because we have determined to be all about glorifying God; when we finally arrive in that "mansion" in the sky prepared for us; some of us will be bloodied and battered and bruised and limping. But by God and by Christ there will be a light in the window and a "welcome home" sign at the door.

Lord, use me. Keep me faithful. Thank You, precious Father. FAITHFULNESS, that Spirit-produced capacity created by God within me. Daily produce it in me. And I eagerly wait to hear my Father's words—*Well done, good and faithful servant.* Welcome home.

Chapter Twelve – Nouns Over Adjectives

Helen shared a quotation with me that has had me thinking. It's an old man talking to a young man—"I won't tell you what to do; I'll tell you what I know." What a great teaching philosophy. As opposed to "I won't tell you what I know; I'll just tell you what to do." And it doesn't always have to be an older man talking to a younger man. I've been learning that an old guy can learn stuff from a younger guy as well.

Rob Bell, pastor at Mars Hill in Grand Rapids, MI has had an impact upon my thinking the last couple of years. He's one of those younger guys. His book, *Velvet Elvis,* has been a breath of fresh air for me. I have recently reread it. While I don't accept everything he advances, I empathize with his being branded a heretic by many "brothers of the faith." He has been misrepresented and misquoted by many "brothers". I've been there! I just thought I needed to open this chapter with that information.

I attended a seminar many years ago by an Argentinean preacher. Juan Carlos Ortiz (author of the book, *Disciple*) spoke with simplicity and passion. He said, "I don't study at the university to get a degree; I am there as a member of Christ's Kingdom to do Kingdom business. I also happen to get a degree. I don't work at Ford Motor Company to earn my livelihood. I work there because God needs one of His soldiers to conquer it for Him. And Mr. Ford happens to support my conquest. But my real Lord is Jesus Christ. Or else I should stop using the name. Jesus asks, 'Why do you call Me, 'Lord,' and do not do what I say?'"

In John 13:34 Jesus said, *Love one another so that all men will know that you are my disciples.* Peter exhorted believers to keep their *behavior excellent among the nations.* It is difficult to make an impact for the Kingdom in isolation. God's plan for the church is for each one of us to demonstrate the kind of lifestyle role-modeled by Jesus in all of our relationships. In doing so, we will have a powerful impact upon a pagan community.

Unfortunately the average church today is considered by our culture to be saturated with mediocrity as well as being irrelevant and just plain boring. That might not always be fair, but it is the perception that is out there. There is a mentality in the evangelical church that has strangled and stifled and strait-jacketed the church in this country for over 200 years. We have made Christianity synonymous with western cultural thought and American patriotism. I enjoy the blessings of living in the western hemisphere and I am a very loyal and patriotic American citizen; but these are not the same as Christianity. We have translated Jesus' words, *go into all the world and preach the gospel,* to mean that we are to westernize the world and, of course, Christianize everything with which we come into contact. At the risk of being branded a heretic, that is not what Jesus has called the church to do. In our minds we have created this unbridgeable gap between the "sacred" and the "secular." The Holy Spirit's work is not limited to Christians and the church. Daniel 2:20-21 says, *Blessed be the name of God forever and ever, to whom belong wisdom and might. He changes times and seasons; He removes kings and sets up kings; He gives wisdom to the wise and knowledge to those who have understanding.*

Look at the context of that. He's not talking to religious people (Read also Deuteronomy 10:14 and Psalm 89:8-12).

"Sacred" and "secular" are categories that enable us to separate "us" from "them" or to divide our lives into "God stuff" and "not God stuff." But these are not biblical categories. The Bible never puts God into the box of the "sacred." He's not just ruler of one place; He's ruler of ALL places.

The greatest example of this is *the Word becoming flesh and dwelling among us.* (John 1:14) I always smile when those negative reactionaries say every Christmas, "It's all so secular—trees, presents, parties; it's just terrible!" Hey, what better time to party! "Yeah, well all of our Christmas customs came from pagan origins!" Well praise to His Name, so did I! What a beautiful example of the "secular" becoming "sacred."

Let me take it a step further; I've already alluded to it earlier. The church must stop "Christianizing" everything. It's a dangerous thing to label things "Christian." Actually, the word "Christianity" never appears in scripture. And the only time the word "Christian" appears in scripture is in Acts 11:26; it can't be found anywhere else in the Bible. It's a noun; not an adjective. It refers to a committed follower (disciple) of Jesus Christ. It's not a kind of thing; it's a person. The first followers of Jesus were called Christians because they had devoted themselves to living the way of the Messiah, who they believed was Jesus. We have "Christianized" everything around us. We have Christian music, Christian bookstores, Christian authors, Christian TV, Christian schools, Christian political action groups (that's an interesting oxymoron), Christian bands, Christian publishing companies, and the list goes on. My understanding is that to be Christian is to do for Jesus whatever it is that you do with devotion and passion. In other words, whatever you're doing and wherever you are, you throw yourself into it because *whatever you do, whether in word or deed, do it all in the name of the Lord Jesus.* (Colossians 3:17) It's possible for music or writing or education to be labeled "Christian" and be terrible. I love what Rob Bell says—"I used to play in a punk band a few years ago. When people would find out I was a pastor they would regularly ask if we were a Christian band. I always found the question a bit odd. When you meet a plumber, do you ask if he is a Christian plumber?"

Quite a controversy was stirred up last year in our church when the sign outside our building was changed from "Countryside Christian Church" to simply "Countryside." It was something I wanted to happen quite a while ago, but unfortunately our new pastor took a lot of the heat for this one. I would have liked to have had our meeting place simply called "The Meeting Place". As a matter of fact I mentioned that during the early planning days of Countryside; but others felt it was a bit too radical. So I really like our place of meeting on 450 North simply being referred to as Countryside. I love it. We got letters and e-mails and a few left the church—"So, we're not 'Christian' anymore, huh?" Let me tell you why I am happy to have that adjective removed. It's an unbiblical title. You won't find it in scripture. The term "Christian Church" has for years been a "denominational" tag with a purpose of separating us from other believers. Our denomination can say all it wants to about our not being a denomination ("We're just Christians"), but if that's true then let's just call ourselves "the church" and be done with it. The phrase in Paul's rebuke in 1 Corinthians 1:12—*I follow Christ,* is not a positive compliment. At the very least we are a "non-denominational denomination." And anyway, the pagan culture could care less what we have written on our signs; but they are very aware of our fruit (or lack of it).

Christian is a great noun and a poor adjective. Rob said that, too.

So back to Mr. Ortiz's statement. It is impossible for a Christian to have a "secular" job. If you follow Jesus and you are doing what you do in Jesus' name, then it is no longer "secular" work; it's "sacred." You are there and God is there. "Christian", biblically speaking, is always a noun; never an adjective.

Rob Bell also said, "I don't follow Jesus because I think Christianity is the best religion. I follow Jesus because He leads me into ultimate reality." I had to think about that for a while. But it's true. All reality is found in Christ. My wife and I were having breakfast together in a local restaurant when she made the statement, "The church has really been our whole lives for the last 40 plus years." It startled me to hear her verbalize it like that. What's wrong with that picture? Now I knew what she meant and there is no one more committed to serving the Lord than my wife, but the words still indicted me. How much of my ministry has been about Christ and how much has been about the church? It is not always the same thing. There have been many times that my ministry in the church has honored Christ and been about the Kingdom. But I know that there have been other times that I have done my "church thing" and the Lord has to be looking at me, shaking His head, "What in the world are you doing, Jones and why are you doing it?" Hopefully, most of my ministry has been more about Christ and less about the church.

Christian is a great noun and a poor adjective.

Nouns combined with verbs are all about MISSION. It is our action for the Kingdom, done in the name of Jesus that defines us, not our labels. What are we doing to make a difference for the Kingdom of God? So maybe it's NOT about the sign on the building. Maybe, just maybe it's all about what the people inside of the building are doing outside of the building. Hopefully it will always be done in the name of Jesus.

Chapter Thirteen – Jesus Over Everything

"my prayer
teach me, lord to walk in your ways
leaning on you, all of my days
open my eyes, to the things that you see
lift my vision to heaven, and off of me
give me your strength, so I may be strong
fighting this war, against evil and wrong
help me to love others, as you want me to do
show me how to do this, how to love like you
lord this is my prayer, simple but true
i don't know how to get there, but i know i need you"
(Written by my oldest daughter, Christine)

> "Remember, Jones…You are not called to preach salvation or sanctification as a priority, but rather you are commissioned to lift up Jesus!" (Personal journal – February 1, 1990)

I wonder what would happen if the only qualification for ministry was a love for Jesus, a passion for God, and a longing for intimacy with the Savior? I wonder what would happen if the job description for a pastor was that he spend all of his time developing the skills and disciplines for loving God? Dallas Willard lists these skills as solitude, silence, fasting, frugality, chastity, secrecy, and sacrifice. I wonder what would happen if the only functions of the church were to study, worship, celebrate, serve, pray, fellowship, confess, and learn what it means to surrender? I wonder!!

But wait a minute. Churches are mini-bureaucracies (some of them not so mini) with committees and boards. The church is a complicated organization that requires leadership and direction and efficiency and co-ordination. Give me a break, Jones. Loving Jesus is important, but it's only one of the many important qualifications for ministry. Right? We don't walk around in sandals anymore (actually I wear them quite a bit). This is the 21st century. This is a new millennium. Hmmmmm…I know that! But I still wonder.

Dr. Richard Halverson is right. We don't want pastors or ministers anymore. We want CEOs. We don't want prophets; we want politicians. We don't want godliness; we want experience. We don't want spirituality; we want efficiency. We don't want humility; we want charisma. We don't want godly authority; we want relational skills. And as a result we have thousands and thousands of churches in this land whose leaders are very qualified to do what the church has asked of them. But the one thing that hasn't been asked of them is to love Jesus. Pastors have never been asked if they love Jesus nor are they in actuality expected to do so. So they don't. And neither do their people.

I can't remember ever being asked in an interview to pastor a church if I loved Jesus. What's wrong with this picture?

As a result, it is not just God who is dead; the church is dead! O Lord, my God, You raise up in this land a new breed of ministers and servants, men and women who are willing to love Jesus with everything they possess, and may they save the church from its worst enemy—ITSELF!! Charles Spurgeon wrote, "The dearest idol I have known, whatever that idol be; help me tear it from Thy throne, and worship only Thee." I remember hearing a speaker years ago say, "My agenda is to pray that God will destroy your lives; some of you are so in love with the world that God cannot use you." It might be good if we stopped using the terms "victory" and "defeat" to describe our progress in holiness before God. Perhaps we should tell it like it is and use more honest terms like "obedience" and "disobedience."

No matter what our occupations are—musician, garbage collector, football coach, preacher—when we come to Christ we all become Christian servants first, and musicians and garbage collectors second. Whatever our "calling," we are preeminently called to Jesus in and through our work. When we have Christ, we have everything! Jesus is either the supreme authority on the human heart, or He isn't even worth listening to!

There is no in between. When I am surrendered to my Lord, I am caught up in and with something infinitely greater than myself. There have been so many times in the last many years that I have personally battled pride in my life. It seems like I spent so much effort pushing it down and keeping it down. It became a little easier when I realized that pride is but the deification of self. On my journey to becoming a more mature disciple of Jesus (I'm still on that journey, by the way) I learned bit by bit and step by step that discipleship means personal, passionate devotion to a Person, the Lord Jesus Christ. I have learned and continue to learn that there is something amazingly humbling in being loyal to Him.

I've sung that hymn over the years so many times—"I Surrender All." What, exactly, does that mean? Perhaps it is the simplicity that attracts. There is no working through archaic lyrics or studying theology or doctrine here. And yet this is not an easy ditty, either. Unadorned in its style and approach, this is one of those convincing texts that does NOT allow us to sing it lightly. "All to Jesus I surrender, all to Him I freely give; I will ever love and trust Him, in His presence daily live. I surrender all. I surrender all. All to Thee, my blessed Savior, I surrender all." (Judson W. Van DeVenter)

What is the will of God for my life? HE WANTS ME!! Jesus said to His disciples, *Come and eat breakfast.* (John 21:12) With these words we are invited to a holy nearness with Jesus. Come and eat implies the same table and the same food. We are truly *brought into the banqueting house where His banner over us is love* (Song of Solomon 2:4) and the only food we can feast upon when we dine with Jesus is Jesus Himself. Shut out every thought and determine to be absolutely and entirely for Him and for Him alone. We give up everything for the sake of the only thing worth having—Life with Jesus.

What is your life? (James 4:14) What a sobering question. Perhaps it is one that I need to ask myself daily. As the scripture teaches me, the only thing that will last is what is invested in behalf of Christ. The only permanent things about life are Jesus and what we do for Him.

Times change. God doesn't, but times do. We learn and grow. The world around us shifts and the Christian faith is alive only when it is listening and changing and innovating and letting go of whatever has gotten in the way of Jesus. Sometimes our cherished traditions get in the way. Sometimes our personal preference and opinions get in the way. Our faith is alive when we embrace whatever will help us be more and more the people God wants us to be.

When the apostle Paul turned the reigns of leadership over to Timothy, he wrote—*You then, my son, be strong in the grace that is in Christ Jesus. And the things you have heard me say in the presence of many witnesses, entrust to reliable men who will also be qualified to teach others.* (2 Timothy 2:1-2) When Moses died, the people mourned for 30 days. Then they put it behind them and followed Joshua's lead. Moses led for 40 plus years, but when Joshua took over the Jordan River parted. The walls of Jericho crumbled, and the nation of Israel went on to victory claiming the Promised Land as their own. God was still with them. He is everything, and He is over everything!!

Chuck Swindoll once said, "When a man of God steps down or dies, absolutely nothing of God leaves." When a long-time leader steps down, the church of Jesus Christ still stands. The gates of Hell will not prevail against it. When I was called to pastor Countryside in 1978, this body was destined to become a great church. I didn't know it at the time; and as I look back, I can say I had relatively little to do with it. It was ordained of God to become a dynamic church and to grow beyond, certainly my imaginations, in spite of me. I believe that Countryside was destined to become a great church regardless of who preached here. This was God's plan for this body and I believe that with all of my heart. And I believe I stand on solid biblical ground when I say that.

Some have good naturedly given me a hard time about stepping down as senior pastor at Countryside. One guy said to me, "You know, there's no retirement plan in the Bible." While that's not entirely true, I strongly affirm that none of us should ever quit serving Jesus until we die. And that's why I don't intend to retire. It's all a matter of timing; because once again, God is in control.

Countryside continues to go through transition and change (and I hope it never stops doing that). But some things never change. Hebrews 13:1-9—*Keep on loving each other as brothers. Do not forget to entertain strangers, for by so doing some people have entertained angels without knowing it. Remember those in prison as if you were their fellow prisoners, and those mistreated as if you yourselves were suffering. Marriage should be honored by all, and the marriage bed be kept pure, for God will judge the adulterer and all the sexually immoral. Keep your lives free from the love of money and be content with what you have, because God has said, "Never will I leave you; never will I forsake you." So we say with confidence, "The Lord is my helper; I will not be afraid.*

What can man do to me?" Remember your leaders, who spoke the word of God to you. Consider the outcome of their way of life and imitate them. JESUS CHRIST IS THE SAME YESTERDAY AND TODAY AND FOREVER. Do not be carried away by all kinds of strange teachings. It is good for our hearts to be strengthened by grace…

These things never change!! Who gave us these things? Who set these things before the church for all times—changeless in the midst of a changing culture? We need to hear more and more and more these days about the sovereignty of God. Why? Because when so little is being said about His being over everything, men start strutting their stuff. God is in charge. Remember that old movie, *God is My Co-Pilot*? What a crock! When did God ever ask to be your co-pilot? He is the pilot, people.

There is so much I don't understand. The longer I live on earth the more questions I have. But one thing I DO understand. God is good; and 1 Peter 5:7 still says *Cast all your anxiety on him because He cares for you.* Scripture teaches that the days we are given and our years are in His hands, regardless of how many and regardless of what we do or do not understand. And in Him we are glad to cast ALL of our cares upon Him.

Proverbs 19:21 says *Many are the plans in a man's heart, but it is the Lord's purpose that prevails!* Once all is said and done, after our plans have been hammered out, prayed and thought through, reworked, decided and acted upon, it is ultimately His counsel that will stand!! The Peterson paraphrase is very accurate—*We humans keep brainstorming options and plans* (and if we disagree with our leadership's options and plans, we shall leave the church—Hmmmmmm??) *but GOD'S PURPOSE PREVAILS!!* I have discovered as I have grown in my relationship with the Lord that God's will DOES prevail. We might make decisions in our lives that are not the best. We might make decisions based upon our own self-interest. We may doubt the wisdom of our direction at times. But in spite of all of this and in spite of us, God's purposes WILL prevail. We might make decisions where we did everything right and for the right reasons but still things don't work out the way we planned. What then? We trust God. He will prevail!! Sometimes we may make plans that seem right; we do all that we believe we are called to do, yet things don't even remotely go the way we think they should (that's been a large part of our history at Countryside). But you know what? The Lord's will prevails. The safest place for us to be is in that trusting, prevailing relationship with Him. It's all about Him. He is to be glorified!!

Our plans may work out beautifully or they may blow up in our faces. And even then we can't be sure that the total decimation of our plans is not a part of God's direction for us. But we DO know that God is to be honored and glorified irrespective of what we might think is going on at the time. We DO know what we ARE to be doing, and KEEP doing.

1. Love each other and care for each other

2. Minister to the downtrodden and poor

3. Live lives of purity and integrity

4. Be content with what we have, storing up our hope and future in the Lord

5. Pray for and follow our leadership in the church

6. And honor Jesus in every aspect of our daily lives BECAUSE HE NEVER CHANGES!!

A friend once asked Martin Luther, "When everyone turns against you, where will you be?" And Luther replied, "Right where I am now, in the hands of Almighty God." So whether you're thinking about your personal life's journey or the life journey of your home congregation, take comfort in these two truths:

1. He will never, never, never leave you

2. WE (I) will never, never, never be in charge.

And just in case this week is a high level stress week for you and when submitting to your sovereign Lord doesn't seem all that fair or fulfilling, take my advice and do it anyway. Later, you'll be glad you did. Maybe sooner.

JESUS OVER EVERYTHING*!!* Yeah!

Chapter Fourteen – Journal Ramblings

As I shared with you earlier, this book has been developed from my personal journals. Reading through my journey, year by year, has ministered to me many times. The following are ramblings and excerpts from the pages of my journals, in no particular order of importance. Some quotes are mine; others are identified where I am aware of their origin. Many of these quotations have ended up in a number of my sermons through the years:

Just as surely as I can receive a salvation I could never earn, so joyously may I hope to realize a ministry I could never achieve.

I've never been in the business of stealing sheep; I've always concentrated on growing grass.

The handwriting on the wall means that the grandchildren have found the crayons!

I've come to realize that shaping men begins with shaping boys.

If the horse is dead…Dismount! (John Maxwell)

We are not great because of what we are…We are great because of what we contain. The secret is this: *Christ in you!* (Bob Benson)

If you ever see a turtle on a fence post, you KNOW he had help getting there.

Human beings are perhaps never more frightening than when they are convinced that they are right. (Laurens Van der Post)

It's always easier to perform something than to simply believe God!

I can't tell you anymore; I've already told you more than I know. (Jay Loucks)

People aren't hungry for fancy sermons or organizational polish…They just want to be loved. (Jim Cymbala)

Two roads diverged in a wood, and I—I took the one less traveled by, and that has made all the difference. (Robert Frost)

We have made ourselves very complicated. (Charles Swindoll)

Before and after everything else, what is our purpose? It is TO GLORIFY GOD!!

Being a disciple means living a disciplined life. And it is not very likely you will get other disciples, unless you are one. (Evelyn Underhill)

He who thinks he has finished…IS finished. (Rabbi Menahem Mendl)

Sometimes we forget that God comes to us, not only to give us peace but also to disturb us.

We're always looking for, or to be extraordinary people…God uses ordinary people who TRUST in an extraordinary God. (Ken Davis)

Tis so sweet to trust in Jesus; just to take Him at His word. (Old hymn)

How many minutes of your life have you really, truly lived? (Tony Campolo)

Perhaps you are more worthless and less fit to live than millions like this poor man's child! (Charles Dickens from *A Christmas Carol*)

All that is necessary for evil to triumph is for good men to do nothing. (Edmund Burke)

Christians are the only people who never have to say goodbye for the last time.

Honesty leads to confession…and confession leads to change. (Richard Foster)

Sometimes the most spiritual thing one can do is the practical thing. (Steve Brown)

It is always easier to follow generalities than it is to follow specifics.

There is an eagle in me that wants to soar, and there is a hippopotamus in me that wants to wallow in the mud. (Carl Sandburg)

Humility isn't believing you're nothing…It is believing that you are nothing without God. (Kathy Troccoli)

I sin because I love myself more than I love God.

Is there any form of belief whatsoever that has taken the place of God in my life? (Oswald Chambers)

The world talks to the mind…A teacher speaks more intimately…He talks to the heart. (Haim Ginott, Israeli psychologist)

I will miss you, Papa…I wish you would not leave…I love you. (Caryn Schmidt; age 7)

Precious flock, Follow my example as I follow the example of Christ!

Don't shoot your own guys!!

It is great to do the Lord's work…But the greatest work is to do the Lord's will.

Say what you mean and mean what you say!!

The key question is not "What would Jesus do?"…The key question is "What is Jesus doing?" (Leonard Sweet)

Big thinking precedes great achievement. (Wilfred Peterson)

The soul is healed by being with children (Fyodor Dostoevsky)

How many of you are willing to lay down your life for your grandchildren? How about your musical preferences?

God's goal is not to make us happy; it is to make us HIS.

You want to be a better leader? Then get a bigger mop and bucket.

To not tithe is to say that I can manage 100% of my money better than God can help me manage 90% of my money. (Tim Baines)

What do you have that you truly believe is really yours?

A right angle is 90 degrees Fahrenheit (Student in one of my classes)

My spelling is wobbly. It's good spelling but it wobbles, and the letters get in the wrong places. (A.A. Milne, author of *Winnie the Pooh*)

Ministry that costs nothing accomplishes nothing!

I came to understand that my preaching must be saturated with the theology of grace.

What any congregation thinks and teaches and preaches about God is the most important thing about them.

Peter preached and 3,000 came forward...He thought he had a pretty good sermon...He preached it again elsewhere and they beat the hell out of him. (William Williman)

Teachers change the world one child at a time. (Plaque on my desk)

Why has the LaPorte, Indiana baseball team done so well, so consistently through the years? Because they do the fundamentals better than anyone else. (Mike McDermott)

Jesus Christ can make opposition to the church a positive power!!

LOVE WINS!!

What small thing can I do today to bring a blessing to someone else?

My grandkids believe that I'm the oldest thing in the world... And after 2 or 3 hours with them, I believe it too. (Gene Perret)

I desire that my disciples (students) live out my teaching – not regurgitate facts…Until they have learned, I have not taught.

I have to constantly "re-educate" myself to listen to God's voice over the chaos and noise of this world.

Real teachers know that they probably can't reach all of their students, but that doesn't stop them from trying.

62 years old today…Still feeling pretty good…Still walking with the Lord…Still seeking Him…NOT wearying in doing good. (January 5, 2007)

Being a disciple has nothing to do with facts…It's all about KNOWING Someone. (Kevin Galloway)

Many times service banishes us to the mundane, the ordinary, the trivial.

If you want to be a kid again, put an orange slice in your mouth, peel side out, and smile at people.

Do what you can with what you have where you are today. (Ethel Percy Andrus, teacher and founder of AARP)

If today were my last day on earth, would I do what I'm doing? OR, would I love more, give more, forgive more…I want to love like there's no tomorrow; and if tomorrow comes, LOVE AGAIN.

And the conclusion of the matter...

Now all has been heard; here is the conclusion of the matter: Fear God and keep his commandments, for this is the whole duty of man. (Ecclesiastes 12:13)

SEASONS OF A PASTOR!! Jesus was an apostle of CHANGE. May the same be said of my life and my ministry, whatever that ministry might be. I love it. Continuing to grow in my relationship with a holy God brings insight into my life. It's kind of ironic. So much of the church of modern times has been reduced from an organism that emphasizes knowing and loving and glorifying God, to an organization that makes us feel good. But regardless of what the church growth experts and emotional health professionals tell us; if we don't know the Lord (as the Lord) and we are outside of Him, we are NOT OK. I'm not all that interested in some obtuse theological debate between Arminianism and Calvinism. I'm not interested in becoming a soldier at arms in the present-day worship wars. The Holy Spirit hasn't led me to get too hot and bothered about post-modernity or the emerging church (actually the first emerging church can be found in the Book of Acts). But I AM committed to proclaiming clearly and forcefully the Lordship of Jesus Christ!

Brother Lawrence used to say, "Let us think often that our only business in life is to please God." It IS all about Him; not about me. We say that a lot around our church. But do we really believe it? Is that a truth in your life; or is it just some cliché? Am I humbled in the presence of a sovereign God who does as He pleases, even when it displeases the minds of men? Do I continue (no matter what) to fall before Him and worship Him because He alone is God? It's just like that bumper sticker I saw a few years ago, "There is a God; and you aren't Him!" Is there anything more comforting than knowing that God is in control?

Anyone who says that it is easy to follow Jesus is either ignorant or a liar. Jesus says that the way is narrow and few find it. And nothing we forgo in the cause of Christ—wealth, popularity, kudos, not even our very lives—come anywhere close to the return that ultimately comes our way. The way of discipleship and covenant commitment and sacrificial worship is costly. Don't let anyone tell you any differently. Just what do you think a disciple (follower) of Jesus is?

- Who are you following?
- Are you a true Christ-follower?
- How many of you are praying for God to show you His will; and you haven't yet obeyed those things you already know?

Do you think that the things that disappoint you are the same things that disappoint God? General William Booth, founder of the Salvation Army, once said to a young man who claimed not to have had a call from God, "What do you mean you've never had a call from God? You've had a call, my friend; you've just never heard it!"

And the reason many of us have never heard that call is because we aren't listening. Many of us are praying to a God that doesn't exist; but rather to one we've created and packaged for our convenience.

I'm not sure that all the stuff that disappoints me also disappoints God. But I do know that what goes on in a lot of our hearts disappoints Him—Disappointment that so many within our churches have not heard and answered the call of God to be committed Christ-followers. Christ's call to discipleship is written large on every page of the New Testament. The problem for most of us is not that we don't know what God wants of us. It's that we know exactly what he wants of us, and it's not what we want to do.

Most of you have had kids. And when Mom calls the kids to turn off the TV and come to dinner, how many times does she have to call before they really hear what she's saying? But there is a mysterious acoustical phenomenon whereby a call to come for ice cream, issued in a quieter voice seems to be heard immediately, and they come running. Jesus calls us to Lordship. And we are quick, like those little ones, to answer the call to ice cream. We are quick to answer the call to His offer of love and healing and forgiveness and significance and friendship. But we are slow to hear His call to do the things we don't want to do—whether big or small—to go to the places that people would rather avoid. We know Jesus as Friend and Savior; but only reluctantly do we obey Him as Lord. One thing I know for sure—GOD IS CALLING YOU TO SERVE RIGHT NOW!!

The church must face the reality of the fact that we live in a global community—both biblically and practically. We are affected by what goes on half way around the world. The church IS to be involved with the homeless in New Orleans as well as a population dying in Africa whether it be from polluted water or disease. As our planet becomes smaller and smaller by way of the internet and the media and jet travel, we have no excuse NOT to be involved. Jesus said in John 17:1—*In the same way that You gave me a mission in the world, I give THEM* (the church) *a mission in the world.* If we are about our Father's business, then we must care about what God cares about. Scripture is filled with His love and His caring for a lost and dying world. It is filled with His caring for the poor and the displaced and the cast-offs of our society.

I know, I know. We have all shared in the frustration of being overwhelmed with the enormity of it all. So many crises, so many tragedies and disasters, so many poor and downtrodden people. What can I do? How can I make a difference? How can I make a dent in the poverty of our world? How can I advance the Kingdom of God in a culture saturated with secularism and paganism? Our family began supporting a Thai orphan when our girls were in elementary school. We began supporting her when she was six years old and continued that support until she graduated high school. She's married today and works for a Christian organization in Thailand. My wife and I support a little girl in a children's home in Jacmel, Haiti today. I've been asked many times, "How can you make a difference? There are so many children like this." The answer is simple—We're making a difference in THIS child's life. Making a difference one child at a time. Making a difference one soul at a time.

There are two ways to share God's Word—preach it and/or live it! Now don't get me wrong. I do not ever desire to negate the power the preached word. I have dedicated the majority of my lifetime doing just that. But the way I live my life and the way I order and project my priorities is a far more effective tool for evangelizing. I like to share the gospel of Jesus Christ by SHOWING. Too often my speaking the word can get out of control. I become zealous and excited and lose sight of God's gentle reminder to *be agreeable, be sympathetic, be loving, be compassionate, be humble...* Blessed to be a blessing started in Genesis and saturates all of scripture. That's our ministry—TO BLESS OTHERS. Jesus' work on the cross convinces me that I can do more for the sake of the Kingdom when I pursue an authentic Christian lifestyle—one that offers blessing and grace and loving kindness and sympathy.

Remember the words of Francis of Assisi "Preach the gospel at all times and when necessary use words." This is how I bring glory to my Father in heaven.

My brother, Doug Weber (former elder in the church where I served) once told us about being on Maui, Hawaii and driving from the airport to the Kanapali coast. He relates his impressions of driving along the ocean, beautiful green mountains on the right, ocean on the left. He relates that as you continue on you begin to see the billboards—then you drive past Pizza Hut and McDonalds. As you drive on and look at the gorgeous scenery around you and reflect upon God's glorious creation, what effect do you think that Pizza Hut and those billboards have? They diminish God's creation. In fact, it can become easier to forget about the mountains and just think about Pizza Hut. Our task is not to be as billboards or Pizza Huts. God wants us out of the way so people out there in the world can see Jesus!! It's not "Look at me!" or "What about me?" Those lush green mountains must be seen in their majesty. Jesus Christ must be lifted up!

Every day I ask myself the question, "Is what I'm doing bringing glory to God, or to myself?" I attempt to filter everything through that same question. I daily admit my ongoing struggle with pride and every morning I talk to the Lord about refusing to accept or expect any of the glory or the credit for anything. I know how easy it is to fake giving the glory to God, and I want no part of it.

I just love it!! An overriding ministry at our church since our new lead pastor began his ministry has been BECOMING. I believe he's hit the nail squarely. The future of our church (OUR future as followers of Jesus) is not about what we're going to do, but rather who we are going to become. What excites you? Do you think that the things that excite you are the same things that excite the Lord?

"He who leaves nothing to chance will do few things ill." Interesting. I can't remember where I read that. And yet, when we rely on the Lord, is it really leaving anything to chance? I don't think so. There is always risk in following the Lord. But nothing is ever left to chance. He who does not risk living in some degree for others, hardly lives for himself; and never lives for the Lord.

"Blessed are the flexible." Very often I seem to sense the nudging of the Holy Spirit saying to me, "You're getting old, Jones; old and inflexible. You don't want to learn anything new and you don't want to change anything settled." And those are the times I realize that I need to stop and talk it over with the Lord. How often can my personal mundane experience develop an attitude within that can begin to warp my spiritual life? When I am so convicted, I know I need to repent, and it is good for me to do so. And I am gently reminded of the words of Revelation 21:5—*Behold, I make all things new.*" As I ponder those words it strikes me that the Lord Jesus is not only making a prophetic promise, but also asserting an ongoing policy—to keep moving with a living Body—and his church is supposed to be just that—you and I are vulnerable to the spiritual experience of biological fact. I am told by physicians that the human body renews itself every 7 years; that the body's cells will renew themselves in a 7 year cycle or less.

Through my years of walking with Jesus I've discovered He keeps me in a permanent state of transition. I wrote in my journal some years ago, "Lord, I don't want to become stodgy, unshapeable, and inflexible. The ongoing work of the Spirit in my life will keep me hanging loose." Someone reminded me of those things just the other day. "Blessed are the flexible," my friend said, "for verily they shall not be broken." A good friend recently made a wall plaque for me saying just that.

As I have used my personal journal to guide me through these pages, I guess you could say I have in some ways laid out the chapters of my life—The seasons of a pastor—Past, present and future. And when I am asked, "Which chapter is your favorite?" My response will always be—"THE NEXT ONE!"

My prayer:

Lord,

I know You are faithful so I choose to serve You.

I know You are loving so I choose to serve You.

I know You are merciful and compassionate so I choose to serve You.

I know You are involved in the seasons of my life so I choose to serve You.

I know You are powerful and trustworthy so I choose to follow You.

You are my Strength and My Hope and my Refuge, a very present help in time of trouble. I come boldly into Your presence, not because of who I am, but because of WHO YOU ARE. I trust You with my life, with all that I am, all that I have, and all that I will become. I CHOOSE to trust and serve You this day and all the rest of the days of my life. Amen.

Printed in the United States
148622LV00001B/2/P